FINANCIAL INDEPENDENCE THEORY

A BEGINNER'S GUIDE

TO FINANCIAL LIBERATION

WRITTEN BY

ANDY Q. ZHOU

FIRST EDITION

FINANCIAL INDEPENDENCE THEORY

A BEGINNER'S GUIDE TO FINANCIAL LIBERATION

Written by

Andy Q. Zhou

Financial Independence Theory : A Beginner's Guide to Financial Liberation
Copyright © 2019 by Andy Q. Zhou.

All rights reserved. Printed with Amazon Kindle Direct Publishing. No part of this book may be used or reproduced in any manner whatsoever without the written permission of the author except in the case of brief quotations em- bodied in critical articles or reviews.

Book and Cover design by Andy Q. Zhou
ISBN: 9781777080907

First Edition: Published December 2019

Table of Contents

Introduction *1*
    What is FIRE, and Why? 3
    The Wealth Ladder 4

Part One: The Millionaire Mindset *10*
    Pay Yourself First 11
    Avoiding Self Sabotage 14
    Assets vs. Liabilities 18
    Wealth Is Abundant 22
    Lifestyle Inflation 26
    Broke Is the New Middle Class 30
    Minimalism 33
    What the Hell Is a Credit Score? (And Why You Should Care about Yours) 39
    You Are the 1 Percent 45

Part Two: How to Spend Money *51*
    The Financial Happiness Paradox 53
    The Value of Budgeting 55
    The Basics of Inflation 58
    Using Credit Cards, the Right Way 61
    Things That I Don't Buy (Or Don't Pay Full Price For) 68
    Things to Spend Money On 72
    Emergency Fund 75
    Dollars Spent vs. Dollars Earned 75

Part Three: Strategies, Tactics, and Pathways to FIRE *77*

Some Definitions 78
Investing vs. Gambling: What's the Difference? 81
Investing vs. Trading, What's the Difference? 88
The Time Value of Money 93
Price vs. Value 94
Quantitative Measures 96
Balance Sheet Analysis 101
Value vs. Growth Investing 106
Trust in the Leadership (Or Not) 107
Short Selling 110
Active vs Passive Management 113
Real Estate Investing 118
Gold and Cryptocurrencies 123
Advantages of Small Investors 125
Bonds and the Yield Curve 128
Stock Options 131
The Buffett Indicator 136
Portfolio Strategies 138
The Rule of Two 140
How to Invest Your First $1,000 142
Tax-Deferred and Tax-Advantaged Accounts 145
The Opportunity Costs of Postsecondary Education 147
Addressing Common Criticisms of FIRE 150

Part Four: Lessons, Stories and Analects 156
Times when Companies Didn't Do Their Math 157
Financial Bubbles and Crises 163
Watershed Moments of Missed Opportunities 170
Impossible Odds vs. the Human Spirit 180

Appendix: Math Stuffs ***188***
    Interest and Bonds 189
    Cryptography and Cryptocurrencies.....................194
    The Prisoner's Dilemma 204
    Linear Programs and Optimization.......................207

About the Author ***213***

References ***214***

Introduction

I got a call from my dad one Thursday evening, and he told me that his car had broken down. I was working a co-op job and taking some classes in university at the time. I had my dad's other car and lived about a two-and-a-half-hour drive away. That day, I was on my way to my evening class, which ran from 7-10p.m., and I told him that if I were to come home it would have to be after my evening class and that I would not arrive home until about 1a.m. My dad told me that unfortunately, there wasn't much choice: he needed the car for work the next day, and working from home was not an option for him. My dad worked for a big Canadian bank in downtown Toronto, but he lived so far away that each morning he had to drive to the train station (about 15-20 minutes away) and take the train to Toronto, which takes about another hour and a half. The whole journey was about two hours each way, so he spent four hours per day just commuting. On top of a typical nine-to-five schedule, he had been doing this every workday for over a decade now. I thought about this situation the entire drive home that evening. I thought it a bit ironic that at age 23, I was actually afforded *more* freedoms at work than my dad, who was 51 at the time. In my job, I worked from home every Friday (sometimes up to three times a week) and frequently left work before 4p.m. Of course, my dad made more money at his job than I did at mine, and I was only a co-op student at the time, but it was interesting to me how people work harder as they age. My dad may not be very old, but he's certainly not a young man by any stretch of the imagination, and the doctor had told him that his commute was not helping his kidney problems, which had gotten noticeably worse throughout the years. The second thing of note is that my dad's situation was not exactly unique, either. Evaluating my group of friends and parents of my friends, I saw a clear trend: although the amount of money they made varied considerably, the thing that they all had in common was the ultralong workday. The mum of one of my friends told me that she had to wake up at 4:30a.m. to commute to Toronto each workday. Theoretically, everyone was supposed to work for around eight hours a day. However, almost everyone I knew worked for longer than that, and once you factor in commuting time, it is clear that the 8-hour workday is truly dead. Say hello to 12-hour workdays. The night of that drive, I was one semester away from graduation, and I wondered if the same fate of the 12-hour day also awaited me a mere four months later. I was left wondering what the point of all this time spent on work was. I have met a select few people in my life who are really passionate about their nine-to-five jobs; they could spend 15 hours a day at the office, even sleep there, and they would be happy. For those people, I say, good on them—to be honest, I'm a bit jealous of them. Excluding these rare exceptions, I think for the vast majority of us it is hard to find nine-to-five jobs that we are truly passionate about. And if you're stuck in this camp, I've got some bad news. The third thing I noted while driving home that night was perhaps the most chilling revelation of all. If you are stuck in the camp of people who aren't super passionate about their nine-to-five jobs (i.e., the average Joe), this is how your life will go: You enter the workforce and get whatever job offer you can find. It is unlikely that this role is perfect, since you've just entered the workforce and don't have a lot of leverage for bargaining. You work that role for at least two years, probably longer, before you get a chance to switch to something more in line with what you want. You finally get that new job and it is noticeably better, but you're still working the same schedule. After another 5 to 10 years, hopefully, you make it into a managerial role. In the meantime, you get married and take out a fixed-rate mortgage on a house that you can't afford. Your old Honda Civic finally breaks down, so you decide to splurge a bit and take out a loan to buy a much nicer car, maybe a BMW 3 Series (or any other midrange luxury car). You have enough money to pay the bills for now, but that may change if you miss just one paycheck. Maybe if you're good at your job, you finally make vice president or some other executive position after 15 to 20 years in the same industry. You wonder whether you've contributed enough to your retirement fund and worry about whether you'll have enough once you hit 65. But you're too busy thinking about where to go for your next vacation in 2 years—which you're saving up for—to truly plan out your retirement. And when the time when you finally have enough money saved up comes, will your boss let you take that many days off work? It's okay, though, because once you retire, you'll have all the time in the world and not be beholden to anyone else's schedule. Once you're 65, you'll have enough energy to travel the world, right? You won't regret that you spent your youth working 12 hours a day, five days a week, right?

Well, if anything I just said scared you, you're not alone. It scared the hell out of me on the drive home that night. It lit a *fire* under me, pun intended. There's got to be a way out.

WHAT IS FIRE, AND WHY?

FIRE is an acronym that stands for "Financial Independence, Retire Early." It is a movement that gained much momentum recently, especially among the "millennial" generation, which includes the majority of the young people currently entering the workforce.

Proponents of FIRE seek to achieve liberation from the rat race of the nine-to-five job and start living the life of a retiree but at a much younger age than 65. At this point, it is helpful to formally define what is meant by "Financial Independence" and "Retire Early."

Financial Independence

A state of being in which one's money (or any material items or entities) is no longer a decision-making criteria in one's day-to-day and long-term actions. More colloquially, a state in which one has enough money to not have to worry about money.

Retire Early

Achieve a state of being akin to that of the typical ideal of a 65-year-old retiree—or regular retirement as most understand it—but at an age of 40 years or younger.

An important thing to note here is that according to this definition, achieving financial independence does not necessarily have a causal relationship to income levels. This means that it is possible for one person to make $1 million a year and still not achieve financial independence, whereas someone else making $35,000 a year may be able to. This can happen if the person making a million dollars a year has expenses that far exceed one million dollars a year, and the person making $35,000 a year has expenses far less than that in any given year. We will touch much more on this in later chapters.

THE WEALTH LADDER

Perhaps, at this point, it is helpful for us to also define various levels of wealth that one can achieve in life. I have consolidated the amount of wealth one can have into 8 rungs of a "Wealth Ladder." Finding where you are specifically on this ladder will help you determine where you need to go.

1. Absolute Dependence

It is my hope that no one above the age of 18 is at this level, although the sad reality is that many people are. People in this group are completely dependent on other people for their day-to-day survival. This is pretty much the case with everyone when we were young and dependent on our parents or guardians for our daily meals; but later in life, as adults, the people who make up this category are often those who have recently declared bankruptcy as well as those who may be homeless and depend on government welfare or charity to survive.

2. Slippery Slope

People in this group do not have enough money to cover their short-term liabilities, such as credit card debt and other high-interest loans such as payday loans. These debts are often called "bad debt" (in contrast to "good debt" such as mortgages, which often have much lower interest rates and carry much longer terms), since they carry very high interest rates and can impact an individual's credit score negatively. People in this group quickly slip toward Absolute Dependence if a solution to their financial health is not implemented immediately.

3. Paycheck Dependent

In this group, people have enough money to cover the minimum payments on their debts and can sustain themselves so long as their paycheck comes on time each month. They often have a mixture of both long-term and short-term debt (as well as a mixture of good and bad debt) at different interest rates. However, since people in this group are only able to make minimum payments on their debts, they most likely are not decreasing the principal owed on their debts in a significant way. It could be the case that they are stuck in a vicious cycle, in which they only make interest payments on their debts, which causes them to be dependent on their paycheck, which causes them to be unable to quit their jobs in pursuit of higher-paying jobs, which causes them to be unable to make anything higher than the minimum payments on their debts. This is a dangerous stage to be in—a sudden large expense or negative event, such as being laid off from work, can quickly cause people in this stage to slip into the lower two levels.

4. Net Zero

This is when an individual has at least the same amount of assets as they do liabilities. This means that the value of what they own is equal to or higher than the value of what they owe. In other words, their net worth is nonnegative. They may still have debt from sources such as credit cards and, of course, mortgages, but they're able to make payments beyond the minimum required amount and are making progress in terms of building wealth and reducing the principal on their debts. They may even have a small emergency fund set aside for sudden negative events such as job loss.

5. Stability

People in this group are relatively assured that they will be fine, at least in the short-term (i.e., three to six months), if they lose their job.

Their net worth is positive, and they have an emergency fund set aside in case something bad happens. People in this stage tend to be older and have had some time to build up their wealth.

6. Financial Independence

This is the level we aim for in this book. As we defined earlier, people in this stage are not beholden to a nine-to-five job since they can sustain themselves indefinitely without working. People at this level often own investments or real estate that passively pays out returns periodically without the owner having to do anything. Keep in mind that the key word is "sustain," which implies that only the bare minimum of life's requirements like food and shelter are being met. People in this stage still do not have enough money for luxurious vacations or fancy sports cars and will have to first graduate to the next level.

7. Financial Abundance

At this level, an individual's net worth is continuously increasing, since their passive income not only covers their daily needs but provides leftover money that the individual can reinvest or spend on luxury goods. At this level, one can do absolutely nothing with one's life yet still get richer as time goes by. Once this level is reached, it is very difficult for one to regress back to lower levels unless poor personal financial planning is involved. At this stage, even a major negative external event, such as a recession, will not cause the individual's wealth level to go below "stability." For those who do fall back down to lower levels of wealth, it is often the case that the individual had inherited their money or gained it through very sudden and unlikely means, such as winning the lottery, and proceeded to spend it recklessly.

8. Transcendence

There are very few people in the world in this category, and their names are generally very well-known by the public. In this category are people such as Bill Gates, the founder of Microsoft, and Jeff Bezos, the founder of Amazon. People at this level can live as if money does not exist. For reference, Bezos was famously quoted saying that he had so much money that he could not spend it all even if he "tried to." Interesting thought experiments can be created for people at this level. It has been proposed that if Bezos dropped $1,000 on the ground, the logical action would be that he should keep walking, since the amount of time that it would take for him to bend down and pick up the money would not be worth it for him. When Amazon's stock price hit an all-time high in 2018, it was reported that Bezos was making about $1,200 USD *per second*. If one assumes it will take more than a second for him to bend over to pick up the $1,000, maybe Bezos ought to just keep walking.

The reader will note that the definition of "financial independence" does not involve living a life of exorbitance or ultraprestige. This is not a book about how to become a billionaire; it is entirely conceivable, even likely, that no one reading this book will ever make it to the Transcendence stage. This is a book about how to liberate oneself from financial struggle and, perhaps, reach the stage of Abundance if one is diligent. My goal is to establish a formal methodology by which FIRE can be achieved through various methods both tangible (such as investing your money) and intangible, (such as developing the right mindset). I hope that by the end of this book, you will have a better idea of how to achieve FIRE for yourself.

Part One: The Millionaire Mindset

PAY YOURSELF FIRST

Talking with my mum one day, I asked her why she had never considered investing in stocks. She gave me the excuse I usually hear from people, which is that she knew nothing about stocks and didn't want to lose money. Hearing this sentiment so often makes me a bit sad, but I'm used to it. Then, she said something that was particularly notable: investing is something only rich people do because they have extra money to invest. In her mind, investing is something she would do only if she had "leftover money." In other words, you put every paycheck toward necessities—your rent or mortgage, groceries, utilities, car payment, credit card payment, cell-phone bill, and so on—and if you still have money left over, you can invest that.

Now, let me put it out there that I love my mum; 99 percent of the time she does know best, and I should do exactly as she says when she says it. But in this particular instance—part of that 1 percent of the time—she is wrong, absolutely wrong. Her perspective is what I like to sum up as a "pay yourself last" approach; unfortunately, most of us apply this approach to our finances.

Think about it like this: If you were to make a list of what you spend money on each month, some things would be more important than others, yes? For example, rent would be more important than, say, that coffee you bought at Starbucks. But if you were to rank the importance of everything you spend money on, where would your "future happiness" lie on that list? After all, investing is by another definition the act of trying to improve your future happiness. The problem is that most people do not put this very important item on the top of the list; indeed, some don't even put it on the list at all. This is a colossal mistake.

The fact is that if you don't invest, you are essentially saying that everything you spend your paycheck on is objectively more important than your future financial well-being. And if this the case, that implies that you are perfectly happy with your current financial state, and there's no need or desire for you to improve. So, why are you still reading this book? Just put it down and go back to your jet ski on your private island. I assume the reason you are still reading is because you want to improve your finances—in which case, hear me out.

I already hear you groaning and see your eyes rolling. You're thinking, "But Andy! Are you telling me to not pay my rent; that I shouldn't pay my bills?" No. No! I'm not saying that. Pay your bills. Definitely pay your bills. I'm saying that you, yourself, are a bill that needs paying. Your own future is the most important bill you will pay each month, and this is the bill you should pay first.

Picture yourself as your landlord but a cooler, sexier version of him or her. You give your landlord what, a thousand bucks each month, maybe more? And he or she doesn't even invite you over for dinner. If you were to invest a thousand bucks every month, you'd build up a decently sized investment portfolio relatively quickly. Practically implementing "paying yourself first" simply involves taking a set amount of money out of every paycheck to invest before paying any other bills. That's it.

Now I can hear a second complaint coming. "But Andy! If I take any money out to invest, I won't have enough left over to pay all my bills." My response to this objection is simply, "Well then, your expenses are just too damn high." Think about it this way. Let's say you earn $3,000 a month. Your rent is $2,000 a month, your car payment plus insurance is $500, groceries are $300, utilities and other things are $200—your income and expenses are exactly equal. Let's assume further that you believe that you absolutely cannot reduce your expenses in any way at this point. All of a sudden, Captain Obvious from one of those hotel commercials shows up and says, "Well, if you spent less every month, you'd be able to invest!" And you say, "Thanks Captain Obvious, but I absolutely need everything I spend money on." Whether this statement is actually true or not is irrelevant. The fact is that in this scenario, you've decided that everything you're spending money on is nonnegotiable and that investing is negotiable.

If your rent increases by $500 a month, you'd likely think, "Damn, I guess I'll have to move out and find somewhere cheaper to live." Now, go one step further and treat investing as nonnegotiable. Ideally, you would be thinking of investing as something with equal weight to rent. That is the essence of paying yourself first. Consider a second scenario, in which your other financial obligations remain the same, except your rent is now $1,500 a month and you're investing the $500 you have left over. And the same thing happens, in which your rent goes up by $500. Your reaction to this scenario should be exactly same as the first scenario. You should be saying, "Oh damn, I need to move out and find somewhere cheaper to live." But most people in this scenario would likely say, "I'll just reduce the amount I invest and use that money to pay rent."

And therein the mistake lies. Paying yourself first means putting yourself in the driver's seat on the road to financial independence, and you are by far a better driver of your own life than your landlord.

AVOIDING SELF SABOTAGE

I went to high school in Aurora, Ontario, a town about an hour's drive due north from downtown Toronto. My high-school civics teacher once described Aurora as one of the top five richest places in Canada; as far as I can tell, he was right. Among the many shining examples of wealth Aurora is home to, Magna International is a large Canadian firm that specializes in manufacturing car components. Many of the Magna executives live in a gated community behind the headquarters building in multimillion-dollar mansions fitted with elevators. Aurora was home to many European old-guard families that have established their wealth and status for one hundred years and counting.

Many people work downtown like my dad did and take the train to work. The five levels of the train station's parking garage would always be full after 6:00a.m. A brisk walk through that garage or down the street anywhere in town would prove Aurora a great place for car-spotting, an activity that my high-school friends and I thoroughly enjoyed. Mercedes-Benzes and BMWs were so common that they weren't worth a second look unless they were super-rare models. Occasionally we'd see something special, like a chrome-finished Audi R8. The entire car was finished like a mirror, and it blinded everyone as it flashed by. There were a couple of Nissan GTRs here and there. Some guy had a McLaren. Another guy came to pick his kid up from school in a jet-black Lamborghini Aventador SV. I biked past the movie theater one day and saw a row of about ten Ferraris parked side by side. You get the picture.

After seeing all those cars, I couldn't help but wonder how people came to amass such exorbitant amounts of wealth. But then, a second thought raced through my mind. Having been born in the People's Republic of

China, a communist country, I was starkly aware of the evils of capitalism from a young age. Even after immigrating to Canada, I would not say that the school system in Aurora painted a very positive picture of capitalism and of rich people in general.

At the time, like many others, whenever I encountered someone driving a nice car, I would immediately think, "Wow, what an asshole, trying to show off." If a young person were driving the car, I or one of my friends would say, "It probably belongs to his rich parents." Worse, if it were a woman driving, one of us would inevitably say, "Probably just a rich boyfriend or rich husband." I apologize, dear reader, for this blatant sexism; please forgive high-school me. I was young and foolish, and my views were unenlightened then. However, notice how I also made these comments without a shred of evidence. Sure, some might have inherited the money needed to buy these cars, and some might just have borrowed use of the car from a rich boyfriend or rich parents—but statistically, it was not likely to have been all of them. What actually happened was that I saw people visibly richer than I was, immediately discounted them as assholes, and moved on. This is a textbook example of self-sabotage.

Imagine you're trying to win the affection of someone you are hopelessly in love with. Imagine that person is Money. Literally, the concept of money personified. Not only are you hopelessly in love, you can't live without Money. You depend on Money for most of your daily activities and for providing you with food and a place to live. You let Money know how great he or she is and how much you think about Money every day. But, let's say that you secretly hate Money. Each time you go out with Money and your friends, you are ashamed that your friends, or even complete strangers, may judge you simply because you have

Money with you. You say nasty things about Money, such as how Money is the "root of all evil" or a "tool used for oppression." Now, how likely do you think that Money would want to be around you? How likely is Money to reciprocate your love?

If you encounter a rich person and your first thought is something negative, it implies that subconsciously—or even consciously—you despise rich people. Logically, this implies that you will never be rich. This is because if you hate rich people, each time you inch closer to becoming rich yourself, you will begin to wonder if you're becoming an asshole. As a famous philosopher from the movie *The Dark Knight* once said, "You either die a hero or live long enough to see yourself become the villain." Naturally, you draw the conclusion that you want to die a hero, so you spend your money to avoid becoming rich. I know what you're thinking. "What are you talking about Andy? I don't spend my money to avoid becoming rich. I spend it on things I need, and I'm just living life as usual." Ah yes, but that's what your subconscious has tricked you into believing. The whole idea of the subconscious is that these things happen without you realizing they do.

Now, I want you to really stop and evaluate your mindset. Are you worried about what people will think of you if you suddenly became super rich? Once you're rich, would you mind if people started talking about you the way you talk about rich people now? Instead of villainizing rich people, we should at least consider how they got rich. If they inherited money, consider how their ancestors got rich. According to *The Millionaire Next Door* by Thomas J. Stanley, 80 percent of all millionaires are first-generation millionaires (i.e., self-made millionaires). A similar study done by Fidelity Investments in 2017 found the proportion of self-made millionaires to be as high as 88 percent! The fact is that the people who get rich from inheritance are actually in the minority.

Now, I propose a thought experiment. Imagine I pick you and nine of your peers from your high-school class and, despite some vehement objections, collect all your assets and your peers' assets and converted everything to cash. I pool the money, then evenly distribute it among the ten of you. I then come back 20 years later to check on all of you and your financial positions. Do you think the wealth amassed by each of you in the last twenty years would still be equal? Or do you think that some will be significantly richer than others? If I were to venture a guess, my answer would be the latter. Intuitively, it makes more sense. The fact that you're investigating techniques to improve your personal finance skills by reading this book increases the chances that you're going to do better in twenty years than your friend Chad. Sorry, Chad.

I should make a disclaimer here that yes, I do realize that being "rich" and being "financially independent" are not completely equivalent—as we mentioned earlier—and that this book is about becoming financially independent rather than rich. However, the pathways one should take to becoming financially independent and becoming rich are essentially identical, so from a practical standpoint, this minor mismatch of definitions is simply a technicality.

You're just going to have to take my word on this one. If you retain your inner resentment of rich people, you will sabotage yourself and you will *never* achieve financial independence.

ASSETS VS. LIABILITIES

The most fundamental breakthrough in establishing a good financial mindset is acquiring an understanding of the difference between assets and liabilities. Perhaps the most well-known definition of assets and liabilities comes from *Rich Dad, Poor Dad* by Robert Kiyosaki, and Kiyosaki's definitions are what I use for this section of the book. That said, for the financial analysis purposes detailed later in this book, we will stick with the classical definitions of these terms in accounting.

Asset

Anything that puts money into your pocket.

Examples of Assets

Stocks, real estate, other investment vehicles.

Liability

Anything that takes money out of your pocket.

Examples of Liabilities

Car, boat, rent, various bills, pets, children.

Back in high school, in grade 11, most of my friends and I had recently turned 17, which meant that we were finally able to get not only a part time job but also our driver's licenses. One of my friends beat us all to the punch, becoming the first in our friend group to get both his driver's license and a part-time job as a cashier at McDonald's. He was rather ecstatic at this situation, and he drove around in his mum's 15-year-old Chevy Uplander whenever he got the chance. It was unsurprising, therefore, that he received a speeding ticket soon after he started driving.

What's ironic, though, was that the speeding ticket was somehow due the exact same day as his first paycheck from McDonald's, and even the dollar amount was very similar to that paycheck. I remember that my friend feeling rather grateful that he had pretty much just enough to cover the speeding ticket and that if he had not gotten the job—or started his job just a few days later—he would've had to come clean to his parents about the ticket and beg them to bail him out. For the next two years or so, he continued to work long hours at McDonald's with the goal of buying his own car one day. In the meantime, he continued to drive his mum's minivan. A large vehicle, it was not great on gas, and his expenses skyrocketed. His mum and he would play a game that I called "gas roulette." The mechanics of the game are simple: whoever emptied the tank would have to pay to refill it. As you can imagine, this incentivized everyone to drive a bit less but had the side effect of having a car that always teetered on the edge of running out of gas. My friend would try to refill the tank significantly whenever he received his paycheck. Living a suburban Canadian high-schooler life meant you needed to go places that were not within walking distance. The term I invented later caught on, and I would frequently hear about "losing a game of gas roulette" as the primary reason for why my friend couldn't come to the movies or a meal at a restaurant. After about two years, he had finally had enough of the minivan; using the entirety of the $6,000 that he had saved up from McDonald's, he bought a 2002 Acura RSX Type S. It was an old car even back then, but it was a two-door coupé, and the shiny blue paint still looked almost brand new. For the remainder of high school, he was forced to keep working his long hours at McDonald's since he was now the primary driver, and being a young male aged 18-25, he was in the demographic category with the highest insurance premiums. Although his sports car burned less gas than the minivan, it demanded only the highest-grade gas, which cost significantly more. A year or so after he bought his car, we all graduated high school and moved on to university. He was forced to cut his hours at McDonald's to only weekends and night shifts, as he now commuted to university, and his daily schedule was also much longer than his schedule back in high school. One day, I came back from university to hang out with him and other friends. I was surprised to learn that he was not driving the car that he loved so much. Upon asking him why, he simply replied, "I had to park it because I can't afford the insurance." I suggested that he should just sell his car then, but he was unwilling to do so. He had spent so much of his blood, sweat, and tears saving up for that car that parting with it was not an option. He stated to me with confidence that he would be able to save up enough money to restart his insurance eventually so that he can get his car back on the road. Seeing that his mind had already been made up, I simply smiled and nodded. His car sat outside on his driveway for the next three years, remaining untouched through three Canadian winters. At some points during those three years, he would get in the car, start the engine, and just let it run for a bit. He did not have car insurance, but he told me that sometimes he would play it risky and take it for a spin around the neighborhood. If he were to have been caught by a police officer, it would have been a minimum fine of $5,000 CAD. Luckily, he was never caught. At some point later in those three years, he turned the key to start the car, and nothing happened. The snow and the constant negative temperatures of the Canadian winter are notoriously harsh to car components such as the battery and electronics. In the end, he did not save a single dime from his paychecks from McDonald's.

* * *

Cars are just about the worst liability one can have. Without exception, every single person I knew who had spent their own money on a car during their high school years ended up being financially crippled as a direct result of buying the car. People usually think of cars as assets, and from an accounting perspective they are. But a car is a *depreciating* asset, which means that the value of the asset decreases over time, making it a liability by Kiyosaki's definition because it takes money out of your pocket on a continual basis.

If one buys a brand-new car, its price is likely to be unaffordable for the average person to fully pay in cash. If one buys an older used car, its components are more likely to break down, increasing the risk of unexpected car repair bills. Consider the average person's monthly expenditure on a car. It is very easy for the cost of everything related to the car (insurance, car payment, gas, general maintenance) to exceed $500 a month (in 2019). Let's assume for the sake of argument that your monthly car expenditure is exactly $500 and that you are making the median individual income in Canada, which is about $33,500 per year according to the census in 2016. Although tax rates vary by region and country, in Ontario, approximately 20 percent of that income goes to taxes, which leaves you with $26,800 post tax. If this scenario describes you, a whopping 22 percent of your income is going straight to your car.

In later chapters, we touch on the power of investing and compound interest, as well as what investing $500 a month can do for you in the long term. For now, just consider what you are actually buying, which is something that is becoming less valuable each day. My recommendation is to avoid owning a car in the first place if you can. Do you need your car for work, or are you simply using it for leisure? If you are using it for work, are you able to move closer to your workplace and save on expenditures by getting rid of the car? Can you bike to work or take public transportation instead? I know that for some of you there are no feasible alternatives to car ownership, and some will legitimately need to have a car or else they'd be unable to work. If you're in this camp, a general rule of thumb is to keep your car expenses below 10 percent of your income, which is achievable by buying a used but reliable car. Alternatively, consider leasing a car. The cost-benefit analysis between buying and leasing can vary from person to person and situation to situation, so I will omit any specific analysis and leave this as an exercise for you to do according to your specific situation.

If you absolutely must buy a car, I recommend buying a car between 5 to 10 years of age. Cars in this range generally strike a good balance between being in a less steep area of their depreciation curve and not being so old that their main components will have started to degrade.

A Note on Liabilities

To be clear, I do not mean to imply that one should eliminate all liabilities. While things such as rearing pets or having children are liabilities in both the financial and legal senses, by no means am I advocating for you to get rid of your pets or disown your children. The key idea here is to get you to think about how to redirect as much money as possible from liabilities to assets.

WEALTH IS ABUNDANT

Imagine that you are the owner of a hotel on the beautiful Greek island of Santorini in 2012, amidst one of the worst financial crises that your country has ever experienced in decades. Everyone you know is in debt, including yourself. There are many hotels on the island, and competition is stiff; you have to make sure that your rooms are of the highest possible quality lest the tourists decide to stay somewhere else. It's been a slow day, but now a man walks in. He is wearing dark sunglasses, a Hawaiian shirt, and cargo shorts. Nothing about him indicates that he is rich until you see his Rolex and hear him boast loudly on the phone about his latest investment in Big Oil; his use of English suggests he does not speak a word of Greek. He then approaches you with a stack of cash that turns out to be €1000, informing you that whomever he had just been talking to had been to your hotel last year, and the person had told him that your hotel was the finest on the island. He tells you that he needs to verify this claim and is willing to put down this amount of money as a deposit while he inspects the room. If he finds it satisfactory, he will stay here tonight. If not, he will take his money and leave. You agree to this, and the man leaves to inspect the room. You are confident that he will find the room satisfactory; the room has a beautiful view of the ocean, and you had just had it cleaned this morning. You are so confident, in fact, that you do not wait until the man returns to use the money to pay back the dentist who had performed a root canal on you last week on credit, seeing as you were in pain but did not have the money to pay for the operation right away. Your dentist is delighted at getting his pay, and as soon as you are out of sight, he turns around and goes to the butcher. Being a dentist these days means that one doesn't make as much as one used to, and he's racked up quite a bit of debt with the butcher for those steaks he's been eating for the past few months; unfortunately for the dentist, the butcher had been in no need of any root-canal work. The butcher is delighted at getting repaid. He waits until the dentist is out of sight to visit a prostitute. Being a butcher is stressful; his income has become less and less consistent as the price of his products has soared, and fewer and fewer of his customers are able to afford expensive steaks. In these trying times, can one really blame him for wanting a little extra love on the side? The ever-so-lovely Katerina had agreed to perform her services on credit, and the butcher is now able to repay her. Having just got back from your brisk walk to the dentist's office, you are surprised to see Katerina waiting for you at the front desk. She thanks you for all the times you have allowed her to bring clients to your hotel and allowed them to stay on credit. She pulls out a stack of bills and happily tells you that she's finally able to pay you back. She hands you exactly €1000. Just at this moment, the man in sunglasses returns from his room inspection. He seems a little flustered. You ask him what's wrong, and he angrily exclaims that his room is dirty and that he cannot see the ocean from his room. He sees the €1000 in your hand and snatches the money away, vowing never to return to your hotel and that he will be staying elsewhere. It happened so fast that you do not get the opportunity to object, and can only watch as the door slams behind the man. You look down at your hands, where a moment ago you had held €1000. You did not make any money today. You take a deep breath and think to yourself, "Well, at least I'm out of debt." Meanwhile, little did you know, everyone else was thinking to themselves the exact same thing.

***

Many people treat wealth as they do any other finite resource, such as food or water. If you were stuck in a desert with some strangers and only a small bottle of water, taking one sip means there is one less sip for the person standing beside you, and vice versa. You'd be tempted to use any means to maximize your share of the water, even resorting to violence if necessary. Many people take this approach to money. If you were to compete for the same job with some other people, your first thought is often a secret (or maybe not-so-secret) desire for the other people to fail or perform poorly at their interviews. We often feel a pang of jealousy when some friend or acquaintance of ours gets a job that pays better than ours or receives some large, unexpected windfall. It all goes back to the same thought: "Well, that's one less sip for me." But this is the entirely wrong approach to thinking about wealth. The fundamentals of economics rely on one fact: one person's expenses are another person's income. Think about everything you spend money on. If your rent were $1,500 a month, and you decided one day to stop paying it for whatever reason, your landlord would be out $1,500 that month. The landlord would have to cut back on usual expenses by $1,500, which means that someone else (or another group of people) would now make $1,500 less that month. And this domino effect will continue. Conversely, if you get a raise and you decide that you want to buy a new car, that is one more car sale that otherwise would not have happened for the car dealer. The car dealer can then use the money they made from selling you the car to expand their business, and the domino effect continues—but in the opposite direction. If we were to truly analyze the situation as a whole, your friend getting a job that pays very well is actually beneficial to you. If people around you are consistently becoming more and more financially successful, this may be evidence that the local economy is doing well, which, in turn, actually *increases* your own chance of financial success. Notice how the argument for cheering for the financial success of your peers still makes sense for wholly selfish reasons (even though cheering for your friends' career successes may be a nice thing to do anyway). The key takeaway here is that wealth is abundant, and wealth breeds more wealth. Conversely, poverty breeds more poverty. We will touch on stories of debt spirals in later chapters, but for now just remember this: generally speaking, when it comes to wealth and financial success, *either we all succeed or we all fail.*

LIFESTYLE INFLATION

"Hey man, can I borrow $200?"

The bowl of pho that I ordered had not even arrived when my friend spilled the beans on why he wanted to see me so urgently. It was a quiet Thursday night; I was in my fourth year of my undergraduate course and trying to hold down a co-op job while going to night classes at the same time. Having just finished a long day at work and a midterm exam a few days prior to that, I was ready to start winding down for the rest of the week when I got the urgent text message. I knew my friend well—we went to high school together. He had bounced around a couple of programs at university after graduating from high school but finally settled for studying computer science at Wilfrid Laurier University, just across the street from the University of Waterloo, where I studied. I knew from my friend's tone that something was up, and I invited him to dinner at a local Vietnamese restaurant.

"May I ask what for?" I asked my friend.

He told me that he needed the money for his tuition bill, but later came clean during the dinner: he needed the money to simply get by. I asked him to elaborate on what he meant, and he admitted that he had run out of money for basic necessities such as groceries. This came as a very big shock to me. My friend had worked part-time steadily throughout his university career. Granted, he had worked only minimum-wage service jobs, but the Ontario government had recently raised the minimum wage from $11 per hour to $14 per hour, so even minimum wage was somewhat comparable to a standard co-op job; mine, for example, paid about $19 per hour. I asked him what led to his current situation, and what I heard over the next hour horrified me. He told me that he had maxed out all his credit cards; in fact, they had been maxed out for years, ever since he started university. He told me that he owed his school residence $3,500 in late rent and, as a result, he could not continue to enroll in classes since the residence was associated with the university, and the latter had placed a hold on his account. He told me that recently he had driven to McDonald's and spent a whole day there. He spent so long in McDonald's that the manager thought his car was loitering in the parking lot, which I later found out was a common problem for that particular McDonald's as it was located in a heavily student-based residential area. The manager had called a towing company in, which towed his car south to Kitchener, about a half-hour drive away. The bill for the towing was going to be $900, plus $65 a day while his car was taking up space in the towing yard.

I was completely blown away by the extent of his financial troubles; I had not noticed any warning signs that anything was going wrong (although retrospectively, as we will soon see, the warning signs were flashing bright red). Granted, I did not have time to hang out with him each day, even though we were both living in Waterloo at the time, but often I would see his Instagram stories and posts about fancy new restaurants he went to or the different kinds of drinks at bubble-tea shops or coffee shops he visited. A few months prior, I had been hanging out with him and a few other friends from high school when I noticed a mesmerizing golden glow flashing from his belt. Upon my asking him about it, he proudly stated that it was a genuine Gucci belt and that he had paid $600 for it. I was a bit taken aback by the cost, and

I asked him if he really could afford it. He brushed it off as not a big deal, and I didn't speak further on it. I later found out from a mutual friend that around the same time as his Gucci belt purchase, he had bought a guitar amp that cost $300. Then, he went to a concert in Toronto. Soon after, he decided to bring his car to Waterloo, which, of course, brought along with it the associated fees such as insurance, gas, maintenance, and parking. At the time, I felt that this move was unnecessary seeing as he did not need his car for work or any productive purposes. He lived across the street from the university and had free access to the public transit system with his student card. Inevitably, all of it caught up to him at some point, and his car being towed was the spark that ignited the powder keg.

After hearing all of this, I immediately gave him the $200 he asked for and also paid for dinner. He ended up paying the towing company almost $1,200 after accumulating some late fees while trying to raise some money. He then got into an accident in that same car just two weeks after he had gotten it back from the towing company. Thankfully, no one was injured, but his car was totaled. I commented that although it was a bad situation, it could be an opportunity for him to finally ease his debt burden a little. One of my other friends had totaled his old Dodge sedan, and the insurance company had paid him around $2,600 to write it off. My friend with the Dodge sedan was surprised to learn that payment was such a high amount, as he reckoned that the market price for the car given its condition before the crash was only about $1,000.

I commented excitedly that the friend in question, can feasibly get at least $3,000 from an insurance write-off if his policy were similar, which would offset his debt burden significantly. "It's like if you're stuck in a desert and somebody throws you a bottle of water," I said. Then came the final nail in the coffin: a mutual friend told me that our friend in question had not paid his insurance on the car, and his policy was therefore void. Furthermore, it is illegal in Ontario to drive without insurance. He would surely get a fine from the police, which is estimated to be around $3,000. He would also be liable to fix the car that he crashed into if the ruling went against him and it was determined that the accident was his fault. After this incident, he acknowledged that he would have to take at least a year off school to deal with his finances, and, in the meantime, he would try to look for a job near his parents' house, as he was forced to move out of Waterloo. His totaled car sat in his parents' driveway, as repairing it would likely cost more than the value of the car itself.

***

Here, we see a prime example of how lifestyle inflation can creep into your life and systematically destroy you. The key to financial independence is maximizing the gap between how much you make and how much you spend. It is a surprisingly simple concept to grasp but something not a lot of people realize. In the event of a promotion and pay bump at work, some people immediately use it as justification for buying a bigger house or a new car. I am not saying that you should never buy a new house or new car, but keep in mind that if you do so—or, more generally, if you increase your expenses at the same rate or at a higher rate than your income—you cannot expect your net worth to increase. It seems so logical, doesn't it? If you get a promotion, it is logical that a small part of you would think, "I'm a manager now, so I should act like a manager and drive a car and live in a house that's appropriate and worthy of a manager." If that's what you want, fine. But don't expect to achieve financial independence.

BROKE IS THE NEW MIDDLE CLASS

When I was in elementary school, I thought that making $100K per year was the definition of rich. In my mind, whoever made that much a year was financially liberated. That was the person driving the brand-new BMW and who lived in a 3,000-square-foot house. They went on vacation once or twice a year and came back with a tan. They went golfing once in a while. They ordered pizza for dinner every Friday. They worked nine-to-five at some big, faceless corporation and selected the least risky option when the time to invest their money came. They wore nice professional clothing to work on weekdays and talked enthusiastically about who's going to win the next football or hockey championship. Despite all of this, though, they had accumulated mountains of debt and would be lucky to retire on time at age 65. In other words, when I grew up, I realized that someone who made $100K a year was painfully average.

I started to question why this is. Why does $100K not go as far as it used to, and how can we seek to improve our situation if we find ourselves making $100K per year or less? I assume this makes up the majority of people reading this book. But first, let us do some simple math to try to understand a typical entry-level six-figure-a-year budget. Say you make $100K a year. The first thing that gets you is taxes. This varies drastically from country to country and across different states and provinces, but for the sake of simplicity I will assume a 20 percent tax rate, which I think is reasonable. So, after taxes, you take home about $80K, which is about $6,700 per month. If you consider the assumptions I made earlier about a typical 3,000-square-foot house in a decent neighborhood as well as a regular car payment on a BMW, the costs add up quickly. I will now justify why I believe $100K per year is not enough to sustainably support a typical "middle-class" lifestyle.

Here some assumptions that seem reasonable to me, with my reference being a suburban hometown of Aurora, Ontario, located about 100 kilometers north of the downtown Toronto core. Keep in mind that I am using data from 2019, a year known for its historically low interest rates.

- You own a 3,000 square foot house with an asking price of about $900,000, with a five-year fixed rate mortgage at 2.39 percent; you had paid 15 percent down in cash. This works out to about $3,100 per month.
- You are financing a brand new BMW 330i or a similar car, which goes for about $68,000 before taxes; this works out to be about $969 per month at a 6.99 percent annual percentage rate (APR). Assume here a $20,000 down payment, a 13 percent sales tax rate, and a 72-month loan.
- Your other car is a minivan or SUV—say, a Toyota RAV4 or similar car—which costs about $40,000. This works out to be just about $600 per month at a 6.99 percent APR. Assume here, again, a $10,000 down payment, a 13 percent sales tax rate, and a 72-month loan.
- You have a family of four, including yourself, and spend about $500 a month on groceries.
- You spend about $300 on transportation to work, whether on public transit or on gas.
- Your car insurance bill is about $150 per month.

- Your utilities, cell-phone bill and various subscriptions cost about $200 per month.
- You're putting away $500 per month toward your pension and retirement.
- For the sake of simplicity, assume that you are your family's sole breadwinner.

For those of you keeping track at home, your $6,700 per month just became a little less than $400 per month. I think most readers will agree that none of these assumptions seem extremely out of the ordinary. Sure, we might argue about specifics—What if we increased the down payment on the house or sold one or both of the cars? What if we negotiated lower interest rates? What if we leased a car instead of buying one? What if we spent less on this or that?—but I am not particularly interested in arguing over specific details, since this budget is purely fictional anyway. The point of this exercise is to illustrate how easy it is for one's expenses creep up to match, or even exceed, one's income levels if one chooses to live a "typical" middle-class life. Note that I have not included credit card debt in my assumptions. This is because the self-discipline needed to pay back credit card bills in full and in a timely manner varies from person to person. Furthermore, the nature of credit card spending tends to be rather miscellaneous, so it is hard to define specifically where the money may be going. Some readers may find it unfair for me to assume that everyone has at least some credit card debt in the same way that people have mortgages. But, if we do assume credit card debt, you can see how easily the remaining $400 per month can disappear; the person in question may even go negative on cash flow each month. I don't mean to scare you, but the math is not your favor when it comes to keeping up with the Joneses.

So, what's the solution to all of this? You're thinking, "I need to make more than $100K a year, then!" Wrong. Well, actually, I suppose it would be very helpful if you were to make $200K per year, but I doubt you'd be able to achieve that in any short period of time, just from a statistical perspective. What if I told you there's a much better and simpler way to have more money at the end of each month? Well, there is. You ready? The strategy is very simple. Just stop. Stop what? Stop whatever the hell you are trying to prove with the big house and nice car.

Listen, I grew up in a family of five in a house that measured 1,400 square feet. My dad was the sole breadwinner in the family, and he drove a 2001 Acura EL. The engine sounded like farts and it would never get featured in any car magazines, but it went where it needed to go just as quickly while being pretty fuel efficient. We bought our groceries in bulk at Costco and sometimes at cheap Chinese supermarkets instead of going to the fancy Italian-themed grocery store, even though the latter was somewhat closer to our house. We would still eat out or order takeout once in a while, but we would always try to save the extra $3 in delivery fees by picking up the takeout ourselves instead of having it delivered. Through all this, I never felt like I was deprived of anything in my childhood. I turned out okay, and financially, our family was a lot better off than many of my peers who had both parents working or a parent that I knew for certain made more money than my dad did. Once again, as I alluded to in earlier sections, it's all about maximizing the gap between income and expenses.

MINIMALISM

"When I get my own place, I'm going to convert to Buddhism," my friend stated proudly as he stared at a giant jade-colored Buddha statue stuffed into a small store at a magical place called "Pacific Mall" in

Markham, Ontario. For those who have never been to or heard of Pacific Mall, there is only one rule about what type of products that can be found or sold there: there are no rules. In my childhood, I frequented the various shops and enjoyed browsing their selections of bootleg DVDs (tells you a little about the era of my childhood) and counterfeit luxury items such as belts and purses (although I've never had too much of an interest in purses). My favorite place at Pacific Mall was the food court, which was legitimately good yet cheap. Coming back to the mall with my friends that one day, I was in grade 12 in high school and a few months away from graduation. My friends and I had walked by a store that looked interesting. This particular store specialized in Asian-themed household decorations. Not only were there statues of Buddha but also statues of other deities such as Guan Yu, the legendary warrior from the Shu Han kingdom of the Three Kingdoms Era in Chinese history. There were paintings, works of calligraphy, and water fountains; you name it. Now my parents, despite being Asian, are conservative Christians who I know would certainly scoff at this blatant display of "idolatry." My household was never one for statues and incense burning or any of that stuff (although we did have some Chinese-style landscape and flower paintings here and there). Although my friend staring at the Buddha statue had gone to Catholic schools his entire life, his family was never as devoutly Christian as mine. Besides, he was half-Filipino and knew many family members who were Buddhist. Feeling a deep connection to his Asian heritage in that statue, he asked the clerk how much it cost. I don't remember the price the clerk gave, but whatever it was, it was too high for someone in high school who worked part-time at McDonald's. So, we quietly walked away. My friend promised to me that when he moved on to university and when he had his own place, he would commit to decorating it fully with statues and fountains fit for a Zen garden.

In the third year of my undergraduate life at the University of Waterloo, I had an international student from China as a friend and roommate. Back then, and even to this day, many of my female friends told me of my gross violations of the latest fashion styles and trends. It's a crime that I fully plead guilty to. I wore plain t-shirts and cargo shorts, with perhaps five dress shirts for the occasional interview or co-op shift. I owned four pairs of shoes, one pair of dress shoes, one pair of winter boots, one pair of running shoes, and a pair of slightly nicer-looking running shoes that I didn't buy from the thrift store, which I wore only when I knew I would be spending a great deal of time indoors. My roommate was the complete opposite of me: despite having moved to Canada as an international student, she had more stuff than a 1960s Midwestern housewife. This brought her into a small but nonnegligible conflict once, when another roommate complained about the amount of space her stuff was taking up. I don't mean to imply that she was disorganized; in fact, my roommate was very well-organized, most certainly more organized than I was (although perhaps that's not saying much). She sorted her clothes and shoes according to the seasons; she had a whole desk dedicated to her makeup, lipstick, and other cosmetics. She would clean the house and sweep the floor way more often than I did (sorry!). It was just the *sheer amount of stuff* that she possessed would have created a logistical nightmare for anyone. If Jeff Bezos ever came to visit her after inspecting an Amazon warehouse, the first thing he would say would be, "Wow, you've got a lot of stuff!" When it came time to move out, it was a multiday operation. When I first moved to Waterloo, I had brought a few large airplane-style luggage cases from home, which I lent to her after I had unpacked and settled in. When it came time for both of us to move out, I asked for them back, and she had told me that that would be impossible. I took one look around the common area, where her stuff had taken up almost every inch of space, and decided she could keep the luggage cases.

***

What does this have to do with financial independence? The answer is a concept I call "associated opportunity cost." What most people don't realize when they buy something is the costs associated with any purchase beyond the price just paid. For example, if you buy a giant Buddha statue that costs, say, $100, the costs associated with it will amount to more than the $100 you spent. The biggest cost, in this case, is the cost associated with storing such a statue. It would take up a lot of space, and if you were living in a place where real-estate prices are high—for example, in the heart of Toronto or San Francisco—then you would be giving up a lot of usable space. Furthermore, there is the cost of maintaining it. If the Buddha statue has some sort of water fountain, then you will have to plug it in and keep it running all the time, which would drive your electricity bill up. Even if it doesn't have to be plugged in, perhaps you'd have to occasionally spend time cleaning the statue, and the time associated with dealing with this is also a cost. Perhaps you think it's not that big a deal to quickly dust a statue off if it gets dirty, but what if you have 10 statues, or 20, or 50, or even more? Consider, at the end of the day, how much utility you would truly get out of a Buddha statue. If you spend, let's say, $1,000 on 10 Buddha statues, and then you spend $1,000 on a new iPhone, which purchase do you think would be more beneficial to your life? Put another way, which purchase will cause a greater increase to your happiness and enjoyment of life?

Granted, you may be a devout Buddhist, and I certainly don't intend to offend anyone who is. Maybe having Buddha statues in your house is an integral part of who you are. But for the vast majority of us, I think buying a smartphone would most likely be a better purchase, both in terms of storage costs and the benefits one would get out of it. This is just one example of doing a mental cost-benefit analysis, but the same logic can be applied to any material object that you own.

Further, what if you decide to move? There are time and monetary costs to transporting a Buddha statue. If you were to land a job in a city far away and have to pack up everything and move in three days, would you be able to do it? This might be a rare scenario, but having a lot of stuff might disincentivize you to want to move in the first place. For one, you may not even have wanted to apply to jobs or seek opportunities in other locations, just to avoid the hassle of moving. My parents often tell me about how a friend of theirs would sell her house and move to a different place when she saw that the market for real estate in her current location had gone up, believing that it was a good time to cash in and move to a place that may be appreciating faster. I asked my mum why she did not do the same, and she said that it was mainly because she did not want to move—just packing the stuff that my family owned would take a very large amount of time and effort.

Notice how owning a large amount of stuff can limit your ability to take advantage of opportunities in life while also increasing your expenses. One potential solution to all of this is adopting the concept of minimalism in your life.

Minimalism

The intentional promotion of the things we value most and the removal of everything that distracts us from the former.

The goal here is to grant yourself more liberty to do what you want without being tied down by your own material possessions. The strategy to achieve this goal is threefold:

1. Evaluate your current belongings and sell or throw out anything that has a has a net negative benefit-to-cost ratio.

A net negative cost-benefit ratio means that you feel that by owning a thing, you're putting into it more time and/or money than the enjoyment you are getting out of it. Get rid of these things immediately; they do nothing but weigh you down. Continuing to hold on to these things is like trying to have a conversation while running a marathon.

2. Look for alternative solutions to current needs that you would regularly be tempted to solve by buying something.

Say you go to the beach and see somebody on a speedboat. Your first instinct might be, "I should buy a boat too." But, as we talked about in the chapter on assets versus liabilities, boats are a huge liability. They are even worse than cars—some people drive every day, after all. If you were to buy a speedboat, how many times a year would you use it, realistically? Here in Canada, the lakes freeze over for six months each year. Is there an alternative if you really wanted a boat to take onto the water? Could you rent a boat for just a day instead? Is there an alternative solution to your problem?

3. Evaluate the benefit-to-cost ratio of an item *before* you buy it.

All of these things about analyzing how much benefit versus cost you may get out of an item should really happen before you even buy the damn thing. Ideally, all of the things that I just mentioned should be part of your analysis.

I know at this point, a lot of you may think that I'm trying to convince you to toss everything and live like a hermit. No, that is not my intention. I have a collection of almost 200 physical books, and it is the most painful thing to move whenever I move into or out of wherever I'm living. However, I have decided that my books are important to me and that they are worth the hassle. So, keep your Buddha statue or buy a boat if that is important to you. I'm not telling you not to. I'm simply telling you to keep their associated opportunity costs in mind.

WHAT THE HELL IS A CREDIT SCORE? (AND WHY YOU SHOULD CARE ABOUT YOURS)

"What the hell is a credit score, anyways?" my friend asked me rather casually. "Wait, you mean, you don't know? But haven't you heard of the term somewhere or heard of people talking about it?" I asked, incredulously. "Nope," My friend simply replied. This man had existed on this earth for the entirety of the past 18 years and had no concept what a credit score was. I should note that he wasn't a new immigrant to the country; he was born and raised in Newmarket, Ontario. Granted, he did not come from a very financially savvy family, but he was less than a year away from getting his high-school diploma and would've gone on to receive it and start his life as an independent adult without even knowing about the *existence* of credit scores, much less how they worked, if not for this chance conversation with me. Not caring about one's credit score is a major stumbling block on the road to financial independence, and this is something that we will fix right now.

The simplest way to understand credit scores is to think about it from the perspective of a lender rather than a borrower. I'm sure in your life there are some people you'd feel comfortable lending your money to and some other people in your life to whom—although you very much love and care for them—you would not lend a single dime unless they were literally about to die. And, even then, you would only lend them money just to prevent their death but not out of any hope that they would pay you back. Thus, you've arrived at the concept of creditworthiness.

Creditworthiness

> *The extent to which a person or company is considered suitable to receive loans or other forms of financial credit, often based on their reliability in paying money back in the past.*

In simple terms, credit is the amount of trust or confidence a lender has that a borrower will be able to pay back a loan in full and on time. The credit score is a metric that sums up a person's creditworthiness in one number. In Canada, the range of one's credit score goes from a possible 300 points up to 900 points, while in the US it ranges from 300 points to 850 points. The higher the score, the more creditworthy an individual is in the eyes of banks and other institutional lenders. There are many factors that affect one's credit score, and we will now go through each of these factors.

Credit History and Timely Payments

This is first thing that banks and other financial institutions look at and the biggest contributor to your final credit score. Banks look at your ability to prove to them that you can pay them back in full and on time. Typically, a good credit history is established by using a credit card and making the payments on time and in full before the due date on your credit card each month. Furthermore, the longer this history of timely and full payment is, the more it improves your score. This can be challenging for younger people who have just turned 18 and have no credit history, or for new immigrants who come from countries where credit cards are not prevalent. My recommendation for people in these categories is to get a credit card immediately and set a low credit limit (maybe in the range of around $500 or less) to prevent the temptation of overspending. Each month, put a least a few small charges on the credit card, such as a cup of coffee or a snack, and pay it off right away so you will not forget and become overdue on the payment. There are special credit cards geared toward people with low credit scores or no credit history. Some companies may require a security deposit and offer you a *secured* credit card, which means that you need to put up collateral in case you default on the credit card's bill. These credit cards offer little to no rewards but are an excellent starting point to establish your credit history with. Remember, the goal is to show the bank that you have the ability to control your spending and consistently make timely and full payments. The goal is not to get a credit card and buy that new TV you've been wanting but can't afford. People often villainize credit cards for getting them into debt, but ultimately you are responsible for your own debt, since you decided to take on that debt on your own accord. Blaming credit cards for your debt is like blaming a car for not being able to drive on water. A car will get you around, but only in specific circumstances and if it is operated properly. We will talk more about the proper ways to use credit cards, and how they are a fantastic tool to get you to FIRE faster if you know how to properly use them, in a later chapter.

Credit Utilization Ratio

A smaller factor than your credit history and timely payments, but a factor nonetheless. The credit utilization ratio is basically how much of your credit you are actually using compared to what's available to you. For example, if you have a credit card with a limit of $1,000 and you're currently carrying a balance on it of $300, then your credit utilization ratio is 30 percent. Easy, right? Well if you have the same $300 balance on that card and another card with a balance of $100 on it and a $1,000 limit, then you must add up all the balances you owe and compare them to the sum of all the credit available. So, in this example, you have a combined $400 in outstanding balance and a combined $2,000 in available credit, so your credit utilization ratio is $400 divided by $2,000, which is 20 percent. This process of calculation is the same for different credit numbers, and I will take a pause here as an exercise for you to calculate your credit utilization ratio right now. Go ahead, I'm waiting.

It is generally recommended that you keep your credit utilization ratio under 30 percent. To illustrate why banks care about credit utilization, imagine that you have a friend named Jack. You know that Jack was never really good with finances and got himself into a fair bit of trouble in his youth due to a drinking and gambling habit. But recently, Jack got a job, and he has not drunk or gambled in a while. You hope that from now on he's got his life together, but you can never be sure. One day, Jack asks you to borrow $1,000. You are still apprehensive, but he promises to pay you back in a month, so you give him a chance. A week later you check in with him, and he assures you that he's still on schedule to return the money to you on time and in full, as promised. A small part of you is not convinced, so you ask him how much he has already spent of the money you lent him. Would you rather he tell you that he's spent 100 percent of the money already? Or 30 percent? The key takeaway here is that in the eyes of the bank, you're Jack. And the more of the loaned money you've already spent, the less creditworthy you seem. The solution could be to increase your credit limit, which will lower your ratio automatically if your application is approved. Or, you may open up more credit cards with different institutions. Credit cards in Canada will usually carry a limit of $500 at minimum to begin with. This strategy may be risky for you if you are the type of person that easily falls prey to temptation and overspending, so this idea may not work well for everyone. The utilization ratio is not nearly as important as a good credit history, so if you have to sacrifice one for the other, sacrifice the former.

Recent Changes to Credit

This factor involves the number of credit accounts you've opened recently. Credit accounts include credit cards, car loans, mortgages, lines of credit, or anything involves you borrowing money from an institution. Usually, the opening of a new credit account such as a credit card will require a credit inquiry. This is when an institution pulls your credit information from the credit bureau, and this results in a small but nonnegligible decrease to your credit score—perhaps somewhere in the range of 15–50 points here in Canada. The effect of opening a credit account will usually disappear sometime after six months to a year (assuming everything else stays the same and you haven't defaulted on any loans), but it is worth mentioning that if you are planning to make a big purchase using borrowed money anytime in the near future, such as taking on a mortgage or car loan, you should avoid opening a new credit account in the near term.

Why You Should Care about Your Credit Score

I know all this talk about credit scores is just about the most unsexy thing one can imagine. "My credit score just went up by 30 points!" is not something one would typically want to hear from their lover during a night of fine dining and passionate sex. But I think keeping track of and trying to improve your credit score is an essential part of the whole philosophy behind FIRE. The main reason is because of interest rates. We will talk more about interest rates later, but for now, think of them as the cost of borrowing money. In this case, borrowing money is essentially taking money from your future self and spending it on your present self. Do this wrongly, and Future You will surely be very upset with Present You, but doing this correctly can actually benefit Future You. The higher your credit score is, the lower the interest you will have to pay on your loans. At first, this doesn't seem to make sense. If I have a high credit score, doesn't that mean I can pay my bills on time, which means that I am in a decent financial position, which means that I have to pay *less* money because I already have a lot of money? Conversely, if I can't afford to pay my credit card, that will lower my credit score and cause the interest rate on my loans to go up, so I'm expected to pay *more* money because I don't have money? Welcome to adult life; that's exactly how it works. The reason why your interest rates go up if your credit score is low is because the banks now see you as a riskier borrower. "Risky," in this case, means that you seem more likely to default on your loan. Therefore, in order to compensate for this added risk, the expected reward from the bank's perspective must also be higher.

But you don't care about what the bank thinks; you want some practical knowledge that explains this whole interest thing from your side. So, let me give you an example. Let's say you bought a $800,000 house with 20 percent down, and because you have a good credit score, you're able to get the rock-bottom interest rate of 2.39 percent per year. So, on your $640,000 loan, over the lifetime of your mortgage, you would've paid $679,438, which is $39,438 in interest. If your credit score were lower and you were only able to negotiate a 2.64 percent interest rate, your interest paid total would be $43,627, a difference of $4,189 from the first scenario with just a 0.25 percent difference in the interest rate. If we bump the interest rate up to 3.00 percent, your total interest paid would be $49,681, which is a difference of $10,243 from the first scenario, all other things being equal. As you can see, even small improvements to the interest rate can easily translate to thousands or tens of thousands of dollars when it comes to big loans such as mortgages. If you're getting a good rate on your mortgage due to a high credit score, it is usually safe to assume that you are also getting a good rate on your other loans, such as car loans or lines of credit if you have any of those. All of these loans combined will heavily influence your financial well-being depending on how high the interest rate is. The way I see it, if you can save thousands of dollars just by using a credit card to buy a coffee once in a while, your return on your time and effort invested is amazing, and this is definitely something that you should do.

YOU ARE THE 1 PERCENT

In 2011, a movement known as Occupy Wall Street shook America. The catchphrase of the movement was, "We are the 99 percent." The meaning behind this phrase was that for too long, the majority of the wealth in America has been hoarded by the 1 percent of the people who make up the richest segment of the population. These people include CEOs, politicians, and, especially, bankers and hedge-fund managers on Wall Street. If you aren't one of the 1 percent, then of course you'd be part of the 99 percent. These are the people working nine-to-five jobs and still living paycheck to paycheck. These are the people being oppressed by the greedy capitalist pigs.

I hate to break it to you, but this notion of there being some grand conspiracy of rich people oppressing the poor is not entirely accurate. I don't mean to downplay the message of the Occupy Wall Street movement. Wealth disparity and the ever-increasing income gap between the rich and the poor is definitely a problem, especially in countries such as Canada and the United States. However, if you crunch the numbers, you may be shocked at what you learn. According to data from 2015, if you make a yearly income of $52,000 USD or more, then you are part of the top 1 percent of income earners in the world. This is an achievable amount of income to reach for most people in the developed world at some point in their lifetime. Even if your annual income is around $28,000 USD, that still puts you in the top 5 percent of income earners, globally speaking. If you make just $11,000 USD per year, which is where the American government has set the poverty line, that still puts you above 85 percent of the world's population in terms of income. Now, I know you are going to say that this comparison neglects the fact that the purchasing power of $1 USD is not the same everywhere, and although most people in the world make less money, their expenses are also much lower. Yes, this is true, and I fully acknowledge this fact. But my point is that if you're reading this, there's a good chance that you are from a developed country where the value of your currency is very high relative to the currencies of some developing countries. Thus, there is a good chance that someone in the world feels the same way about you as you might feel toward the richest 1 percent of people in your own country. During my time at the University of Waterloo, I had many co-op jobs that, when added together, paid a salary in the neighborhood of about $37,000 CAD each year. I was quite ecstatic when I first received such a job offer in my first year of undergraduate education but felt almost cheated by the time I got to my third year and landed a co-op job at a different company that paid the exact same amount. The median individual annual income in Canada when I was a third-year undergraduate was about $35,000 CAD per year. I was making as a co-op worker what the average Canadian made as a full-time worker. I realized that the problem was that my expectations had changed, and it was that fact in and of itself that made me less happy. When I realized this, I began to notice that some of my peers were making a lot more money than I but experiencing similar frustrations. At Waterloo, it was not uncommon for a student in a high-demand field such as computer science or engineering to make over $100,000 USD per year on their co-op terms. The jobs that paid that much were mostly located in California, and it was something of a rite of passage for someone in computer science to experience an internship there. Those that did not make it to California would still often find jobs in Canada, which paid significantly less—maybe in the neighborhood of $60,000 to $80,000 CAD per year. Simply put, even those that did not make it to California often still had jobs that paid double as a co-op position what the average Canadian full-time worker would make. But inevitably, my peers in computer science who were forced to "settle" for a job that paid $60,000CAD per year would often lament to me that they felt defeated and hopeless. My point is to illustrate that often we exist within our own "bubbles," and sometimes it may be helpful for us to try and escape our bubbles and reset our own frames of reference. What we call the "1 percent" can naturally be further divided into "pretty rich," "mind-numbingly rich," and "richer than God," and each of these groups lives in its own bubble, wherein the 1 percent would feel jealous of the 0.1 percent, and so on. I would argue that for the most part—with some exceptions, of course—rich people did not gather and conspire against the poor the same way that you did not gather all your friends to conspire against some cobalt miners in the Democratic Republic of the Congo. Life can be unfair sometimes, and we should acknowledge the privilege that we have as members of one of the top income brackets in the world. If you still need yet another reason why FIRE is something that is worth trying to achieve, an altruistic reason could be to use your free time and extra money to help other people. In a developed country such as Canada or the United States, we are in a uniquely advantageous position to use our strong currencies to make a large amount of impact in the world by donating to charitable causes or otherwise funding projects that we are passionate about. Imagine the amount of social impact you can make if you had lots of time and money and weren't tied down to a nine-to-five job. Certainly, this has served as part of my own motivation for achieving FIRE, and perhaps it can be part of yours as well.

It's a Lonely World

If you're trying to achieve FIRE in a modern, developed country, you may feel a sense of loneliness that comes from more than just the fact that you're in the top 1 percent of income earners globally. Although we have just discussed various ways for one to save money and live frugally, that alone will not be enough. Unless you are born wealthy or have some unique talent that very few people have, to achieve FIRE you *must* invest in one thing or another, whether this is stocks, real estate, or your own business—and you must be good at it, too. The fact is, most people don't achieve FIRE, and most people are not good at investing. Therefore, your goal is to be different than everyone else, which will inevitably bring about waves of loneliness from time to time. Being a good investor is the equivalent of being a contrarian. If you look at the most successful investments or business ventures of famous people, you will find almost without exception all of them went against the popular opinion on something. Either someone put their money in an early Apple when everyone thought that the company was going to tank or someone started an online store selling books when brick-and-mortar retail dominated the world, and people didn't understand how the Internet worked. It could even be something unrelated to business or finance. At any given time there probably exists fewer than 50 people in the entire world who truly understand the full extent of the theories proposed by Stephen Hawking or Albert Einstein in physics and mathematics. Imagine that you are one of the 50 who do; chances are, not even your closest friends or family would be able to fully relate to what you know and how you feel. Whenever you propose a new mathematical theory, people may just look at you and nod their heads slowly, then go back to talking about the latest sports game. In investing, we often try to seek assurance from others that we are putting our money to good use, whether we are buying a stock, buying a house, or starting a business. You will most likely be disappointed in your quest for assurance, as people will just smile and nod as if you were trying to explain a very complicated math equation to them. Do not be discouraged by this; take this as a sign that you are well on your path to achieving your goals.

Part Two: How to Spend Money

You remember that one weird kung fu movie with Jackie Chan and Jet Li called *The Forbidden Kingdom*? In case you don't, let me jog your memory. In the movie, the main protagonist, Jason from South Boston, gets chased by some thugs; while running away, he holds a magical staff belonging to the Monkey King. He gets teleported to a different time (another dimension?) in ancient China, where he meets Jackie Chan, who plays a drunken kung fu master (as in, he's only good at kung fu if he's drunk? I guess?). Jackie Chan promises to teach Jason the true way of kung fu. Anyway, the plot itself isn't the most important, but what matters is one particular scene. In that scene, Jackie Chan pours Jason some tea and continues to fill his cup even when it begins to overflow, and causing Jason to scald his hand on the hot water. He then turns to Jason and says, "How can you fill your cup when it's already full? How can you learn kung fu, when you already know so much?"

Trust me, there is a reason why I brought up some random kung fu movie that got a 60 percent score on Rotten Tomatoes. In this part of the book, I want to teach you how to spend money. Now, I can already sense the incoming wave of torches and pitchforks coming my way. I know you're about to yell at me, "How dare you try to tell me how to spend my own money? It's *my* hard-earned money!" But put away the pitchfork for a second and hear me out. I know you believe that you are already spending your money in the most optimal way, one that maximizes your happiness, but the evidence just doesn't back up that claim. People make impulse purchases; people buy liabilities that cost them more money down the line; people splurge on items that they regret buying later. I would argue that most people do not spend their money properly, and, statistically speaking, you are more likely to be in this group than not. In fact, I will even go one step further and claim that the biggest hurdle for most people to achieving financial independence is not a lack of income but an inability to properly audit their expenses.

I want you to forget everything (if only temporarily) you think you know about how to optimally spend money. Let me put on my best Jackie Chan impression. How can I fill your cup when it is already full? How can you expect to maximize your savings and investments without reducing your spending? You can't. You need to empty your cup before I can fill it.

THE FINANCIAL HAPPINESS PARADOX

Remember my friend, the one with the 2002 Acura RSX Type S that he bought with the money he had saved up in high school working at McDonald's? I tried to convince him to sell it as he had parked it on his driveway, since he couldn't afford the insurance. I told him that if he were to sell his car, he could take the money and put it anywhere, under his mattress if he wanted, and then just buy a nicer car for the same amount of money a few years later when he graduated from university and got a full-time job. His retort to me was simple and one that I had no response to. He told me that he simply had no desire for another "nicer" car. Even though his car was 15 years old at the time, in his mind, it was everything that he had ever wanted in a car. Not that he would say no to a free Ferrari if somebody wanted to give him one, but in his mind, he had achieved his goal of getting himself a nice car already. There was no need to go further. Although I still felt that he was not making the most optimal financial decision, I nodded and clapped him on the back; I had to respect that. Financial independence is all about getting yourself to the point where you do not feel the need to go further in improving your financial situation, because you're already in a good enough position.

But then I thought about it, and I arrived at something of a paradox. Most people, my friend included, would say that all the things they spend money on are worth it and necessary, yet simultaneously complain that they do not have enough money left over at the end of the month, even taking on further debt. In order for both of the previous statements to be true, the following would have to be true:

1. Every single purchase they make maximizes their happiness to a degree greater than saving or investing the money instead of spending it would have.
2. Having a net worth that does not increase also maximizes their happiness, if that's what allows them to make all their current purchases—because, as stated in the previous point, all their purchases maximize their happiness.

In essence, what I mean is that if there's truly nothing you can cut from your spending because everything you spend money on is "worth it," you shouldn't be complaining about debt or not having enough money, because the benefit of making your existing purchases is greater than the cost you're paying in terms of possible debt or the work you put in to acquire that money in the first place. This means, then, that you'd be completely happy with your current financial situation, but that's not the case with most people. Hence, a paradox.

The solution to this paradox is simple. The first statement is pretty much always untrue for almost everyone. People generally benefit in terms of happiness if they spend a little less and save or invest the difference for their own futures. The problem is that humans are irrational, and we only see our current needs and desires; we work actively to fulfill those instead of thinking about what our future selves would want. I want to break this cycle, and you already have the first key, which is recognizing this paradox. The second key to breaking the cycle is budgeting.

THE VALUE OF BUDGETING

If I were to print out all your credit card and bank statements for the past three months and lay them out in front of you, and we were to go auditing your expenses line-by-line, how well would you be able to justify each and every expense? Maybe "justify" is the wrong word; it feels accusative, which is not my intention at all. Put differently, if we went through all your expenses, would you say that each expense was necessary—or worth it, at least? Would there be any items you think you could have spent less money on and still maintain a lifestyle relatively equal to what you enjoy now? This is essentially the first step that any professional personal finance advisor will do if you hire one for help. However, I think this step is so easy that you can do it yourself right now, for free. The expense you pay for a personal finance advisor is the first thing you can cut from your budget (assuming you don't have more complicated financial issues). Thank me later.

There exists a myriad of free budgeting software programs, such as Mint.com, which you can connect your bank accounts to; the platform will refresh the data automatically and display it using charts and graphs as well as list and categorize your expenses. If you are wary of using online tools, you can even use something as simple as an Excel sheet that you store locally and encrypt with a password. Despite this being so simple, it often surprises me how few people actually take the time to budget. If one wanted to cook some pasta for dinner, for instance, most people would open their fridge and take inventory of what they have, then go out to buy a missing ingredient or switch to making something else. Notice that when it comes to cooking, we are often very aware of what we need or don't need and the steps we need to take to acquire the required resources if we need something that we don't have. So, just take that logic and extend it in a general sense when it comes to money. If one reaches a state wherein one has a perfect understanding of how much money one has and where it goes every month, it becomes much easier to plan out the next step to achieving a better financial future. Think of your money as the amount of raw cooking ingredients you have and becoming financially independent as making the perfect plate of pasta.

If you wish to become financially independent, you must budget. Trying to achieve FIRE without budgeting is like trying to go on a road trip somewhere far away without a GPS or even a paper map, driving aimlessly in the general direction of where you want to go. If you somehow end up where you want, it will simply be a product of pure chance. In general, chances are that you will not get to your destination at all. This makes it a horrible strategy to adopt, yet many choose not to budget when it comes to their finances.

Budgeting Techniques

Let's go through some practical ways to budget. Once you've determined where each and every penny you spend actually goes, it is time to cut out some things that you are spending money on that may be unnecessary, such as subscriptions to services you no longer use or don't get the full benefit of. For instance, that gym membership you signed up for on impulse but never use. You may want to draft up a list of the five things you spend the most money on each month and compare them to the five things that you want to spend money on that are important to you. For example, say your car expenses are in the top five things you spend the most money on each month (chances are that this is the case for most people who have a car); is having that particular car in the list of the top five things that are the most important to you? In other words, are you satisfied with the amount you are spending on it, or would you be happier downgrading to a cheaper car and saving the difference or even selling that car altogether? You can apply the same logic with just about anything. Rent, coffee, subscription services, and so on.

One way to motivate yourself to save more money is to track your net worth. Your net worth is the total amount of wealth you have after you add up all your assets and subtract all your liabilities. Note that when I talk about assets and liabilities here, I am using the traditional definition in accounting and not the Kiyosaki definition that we have been using so far. So, in this sense, a car would be an asset. Also note that your net worth can be positive, zero, or negative. Essentially, if you owe more than you own, then your net worth is negative, and vice versa. Like most university students, my own net worth remained negative all throughout my university life due to student debt. I interned at various companies during university, and physically seeing my net worth increase with every paycheck, as displayed by my budgeting software, was one of the biggest motivating factors for me to keep saving. I remember at one point I opened up my budgeting software and saw that my net worth had peaked at the highest it had ever been since I started tracking: a whopping −$14,358. I set a goal for myself right there and then to hit a net worth of $0 within the next 18 months. To me, it was crazy to think that when a person is born their net worth is $0, but throughout the years it actually can go down. I realized that I was actually worth less than the day I was born in terms of wealth, and that was a big revelation for me at the time. Some of you may have a similar net worth or even less than I had on that day. If that person is you, I hope it is also somewhat of a revelation for you. As you work your way up, I think it's important to celebrate important milestones in your net worth, such as $0, $10,000, $100,000, and so on; this will help you stay on track.

THE BASICS OF INFLATION

I know this one guy who is a friend of a friend. The man had a general distrust of authority that was not limited to just teachers and law enforcement. His distrust extended to the banking system, so he kept all his money in cash in his house. My mutual friend tells me that he had once been screwed over by some bank fees that he was not aware of and, after that, he did not trust the bank to safeguard his money. In his mind, the best way to ensure that his money preserved the highest proportion of its value in the safest way was to keep it beside him physically. He did not realize that by doing so, he was exposing his money to a disease that slowly causes his wealth to degenerate over time. That disease is called inflation.

Inflation

A sustained increase in the general price level of goods and services in an economy over a period of time.

You remember your parents telling you how much shit they could buy with a dollar when they were young? If you were to talk to your grandparents about this, chances are they wouldn't even be talking in terms of dollars; you could buy a Coke for 10 cents back then. At first, the younger you must have thought about how you'd be rich if you had lived back then. If you could buy a car for $500 or a house for $10,000, you'd be there in no time. Everyone back then must have been rich, right? Well, no. The problem is although things cost less back then, people also made a lot less money. In other words, the number printed on a banknote doesn't really matter—what matters is how much you can buy with that banknote. This illustrates the concept of purchasing power.

Purchasing Power

The value of a currency expressed in terms of the amount of goods or services that one unit of money can buy.

For example, say you wanted to buy a loaf of bread. If one loaf of bread cost $1, and you made $1 an hour, you'd have to work for an hour to buy that loaf of bread—simple. Alternatively, if the same loaf of bread cost $10, but you made $10 per hour, you'd be in the exact same situation as in the first scenario, albeit with different numbers. If you made $10 per hour and a loaf of bread were $1, then your purchasing power would be 10 times higher, and you'd be much better off compared to the previous scenario. As you can see, the numbers don't matter; all you care about in the end is purchasing power.

If you wanted to be a trillionaire, there is no need for you to look further than Zimbabwe back in 2008. Having gained independence in the 1980s, in the late 1990s the then president of Zimbabwe, Robert Mugabe, embarked on a series of economic reforms that proved disastrous for the country. A series of land redistribution policies put many people who had very little to no experience in farming in charge of farmland. This resulted in a rapid decline in food production, which caused the banking sector to collapse and the unemployment rate to skyrocket. The situation was not helped in the least by Zimbabwe's involvement in the Second Congo War and the subsequent waves of economic sanctions from countries in the European Union and the United States, all of which had grown wary of Mugabe's dictatorial ways. To combat the rapid decrease in purchasing power of the Zimbabwe Dollar, the Reserve Bank of Zimbabwe elected to begin printing more money. This, of course, had the opposite of the desired effect, as the move simply devalued the Zimbabwe Dollar at an even faster pace. Inflation became hyperinflation. The peak month of hyperinflation occurred in mid-November 2008, with an inflation rate estimated at 79,600,000,000 percent per month. This resulted in $1 USD becoming equivalent to the staggering sum of over $2.6 billion Zimbabwe Dollars. The problem became so bad that the computer systems in banks would glitch due to the staggeringly large numbers they were being required to handle. Zeroes would sometimes have to be manually added to receipts when these glitches occurred. Bankers would sometimes have to represent account balances in scientific notation, a method typically used by scientists when dealing with numbers in extreme magnitudes of scale. Banks were forced to keep reissuing banknotes of higher and higher denominations; the year of 2008 eventually ended with the highest denominated note worth one hundred trillion Zimbabwe Dollars—or the same value as around $0.40 USD at the time. This banknote would later become somewhat of a novelty and fetch much higher prices on websites such as eBay as a collectible and a demonstration of what can go wrong if inflation is not kept in check. The decade following the Zimbabwe Dollar's hyperinflation would see a complete loss of faith in the Zimbabwe Dollar. Today, most Zimbabweans transact with US Dollars or the South African Rand.

Barring periods of hyperinflation, a small amount of inflation is a natural consequence of a growing economy. As more people start buying more goods and services, the demand for those goods and services increases, which in turn drives up the price for those goods and services. We will refrain from going too deep into the types and causes of inflation and details about monetary policy, since understanding the specifics of exactly how inflation works is not crucial to achieving FIRE. But, in general, note that inflation occurs naturally. Looking at the historical data, we can assume that in developed countries such as Canada or the United States, inflation tends to hover at around 2 percent per year. This means that if you were to keep all your money in cash in your house or in an account that pays little to no interest, you would lose about 2 percent of that cash's purchasing power each year simply due to degradation by inflation. This rate of 2 percent is only an estimate and can vary depending on economic conditions, but I hope to illustrate the fact that one must think about safeguarding themselves from inflation if they wish to achieve FIRE. We will detail strategies on precisely how to do this in part 3 of this book.

USING CREDIT CARDS, THE RIGHT WAY

I got my first credit card when I was 18. Unlike most people, though, ever since my first day with a credit card I have always been careful not to rack up interest on credit card debt. Here in Canada, the interest rates for a credit card typically start at around 20 percent. I grew up reading and hearing about stories of people who have crippled themselves financially with credit card debt, and I was determined not to be a case study. Perhaps because I grew up in a family that did not have a lot of money, I was forced to think about what kinds of things were good purchases and what kinds were wastes of money since a young age. Both then and now, I deeply hold the belief that paying a high interest rate is one of the worst ways to waste your money. For this reason, ever since the day I got my first credit card, I have not paid a single dime of credit card interest in my life, ever. I don't say this as some sort of weird flex; I'm telling you this because I think if an 18-year-old suburban Canadian high schooler who came from a family of poor immigrants can successfully avoid all credit card debt, so can you. But before I go any further, let me tell you why you should use a credit card instead of any other payment method whenever possible.

Credit Cards vs. Debit Cards vs. Cash

I have already addressed the potential benefit to improving one's credit score by using a credit card, but there is a far more important reason why I always use a credit card over debit or cash whenever possible. You guessed it: the rewards. Credit cards often give rewards such as cashback or travel credits simply for using the card. The specifics of each reward program are subject to change, so make sure to do your own research for the most up-to-date information. Although, in general, I think it is safe to say that even the most basic credit card will offer about 1 percent cashback (or some type of travel credit equivalent to 1 percent cashback) on just about everything, with no annual fee. This may not sound like much, but if you can pay for large expenses such as your utilities bill—money that you were going to spend anyway—with a credit card, paying for these purchases in cash is literally leaving money on the table. Many credit cards will offer a substantial signup bonus just for opening an account, and the value of these offers can go up to several hundreds of dollars. It is worth noting at this point that you should never increase your spending just for the sake of getting credit card rewards. The correct way to collect rewards is to simply replace your current spending on debit and cash with payments on a credit card. This way, you can ensure that your expenses do not increase and still receive the benefits that you would've otherwise missed out on by using a debit card.

Another benefit to using credit cards is the reduced exposure to the risk of financial fraud. Whenever you pay with a debit card, the sum of the purchase is immediately withdrawn from your account. This exposes you to a greater financial risk if the charge on your debit card is fraudulent, because almost all banks and credit card issuers have a zero-liability policy on their credit cards. This means that if your credit account is compromised and a fraudulent charge occurs, the bank will refund you the money and investigate the fraudulent charge themselves. However, since you, the customer, have already received your refund, you are no longer liable for or exposed to any financial risk. And, quite frankly, you don't have to care whether the bank got their money back, because it is their problem now. The same is not true if you had used a debit card. For debit cards, the money is taken directly out of your account. In a similar scenario in which a fraudulent charge occurs, banks will try their best to locate your money, but if they cannot do so, you are on the hook for your lost money and may not ever get it back. I believe I do not need to mention anything about cash. If you paid someone in cash and they ended up defrauding you, better start praying to your preferred deity that you get it back.

A smaller but nonnegligible benefit of credit cards is that they allow you to have access to a greater amount of cash temporarily. Think about this scenario: Let's say you need to pay your utilities bill soon, and your rent is also due a few days later. Let's say you can pay for your utilities with a credit card but your rent must be paid in cash; assume that you currently do not have enough money for both but will have enough money in two weeks, when you get your paycheck. If you have a credit card, you can simply pay for the utilities using credit; assuming that now you have enough cash to pay your rent, you've just avoided both getting evicted and getting your water shut down. And if you pay off the credit card debt when your paycheck arrives in two weeks, you will avoid any credit card interest. If you do not have a credit card, you may have to choose between paying your rent or paying your utilities bill simply because you don't have enough cash for both. To illustrate the importance of having cash, it is helpful to approach it from an accountant's perspective and imagine yourself as a company. In accounting, it is often very important to not only keep track of a company's revenues and profits but also its cash flow. A company without cash will instantly go bankrupt, whereas companies that are consistently unprofitable can stay in operation for years, sometimes even for longer than a decade. Imagine a scenario in which you run a bar and you allow your customers to run up a tab, letting it go unpaid for a long time. On paper, your revenues are through the roof. You have a ton of people that owe you money that you can theoretically collect on. But, in reality, if your customers don't pay you soon, your expenses will rack up and bankrupt you. Your suppliers, landlord, employees, and so on are unlikely to be equally generous in letting their goods and services go unpaid for a long time. Returning to the topic of credit cards, the month or so of interest-free borrowing before your credit card bill is due provides you something of a safety net in case something happens that causes you to run out of sufficient cash for less than a month.

Some credit cards offer smaller perks such as travel insurance or access to airport lounges, or special invites to events such as concerts and movies. These perks vary drastically from card to card, so I will simply mention that they exist. You will need to check the benefits package of your specific credit card to find out more.

By now, I've hopefully convinced you why you should have at least one credit card. However, I know some of you may already be in credit card debt or have recently climbed out of it after a long struggle. To those in the first camp, I will talk about strategies to help you reduce that debt. If you're in the second camp, I implore you to give credit cards another try unless you absolutely know that you lack the self-control needed not to overspend. That being said, if you want to achieve FIRE, having this type of self-discipline is essential.

Tiers of Credit Cards

I have broken down the different types of credit cards into five tiers, which I've labelled "A" to "E," with "A" being the best and "E" the worst. For this section, I will actually name specific examples to illustrate the contrast between the different tiers, but note that these may be subject to change in the future.

A. Exclusive, invite only

These cards are impossible to apply for and only available via invitation. To receive the invite, the cardholder will often have to meet a minimum-net-worth requirement as well as an annual minimum spending amount. As a result, these cards are only available to individuals with very high net worth. The cards often have extremely high annual fees but provide exclusive perks such as a personal concierge and no credit limits. Examples include the American Express Centurion ("The Black Card"; worldwide) and the JP Morgan Chase Reserve ("The Palladium Card"; US)."

B. Prestigious, high annual fee

These cards are accessible to all who have a high enough credit score, but they are usually targeted toward frequent travelers and wealthy individuals. These cards often carry a high annual fee, in the range of hundreds of dollars per year. Benefits can include access to airport lounges, travel credits, and other rewards. Examples include the American Express Platinum (Canada, US, UK) and Chase Sapphire Reserve (US)

C. Low annual fee, good rewards

This is probably the most common type of credit card. These typically have annual fees of around $100 and offer better rewards than what you would otherwise get with a no-annual-fee card; cardholders typically enjoy at least 2 percent cashback (or the equivalent in points) on everything with higher rewards for certain categories. Examples are too numerous to name.

D. No annual fee, low rewards, entry level

These cards are great for beginners, students, and those with a limited credit history or lower credit score to start building up their credit history and make their way up to cards that give a higher rate of reward. They are a great entry point for people who may not qualify for a higher-tier credit card. Typically, these will still net you at least 1 percent cashback or equivalent on everything, and they may also have bonus categories with higher rewards. Examples include the Tangerine Cashback Mastercard (Canada) and American Express Everyday Card (US)

E. No rewards, no annual fee, designed for balance transfers and people with low credit scores, secured cards

These cards are designed for people who have absolutely no credit history or who are in the process of rebuilding their credit scores after damaging them with previous missed payments on debt. Although these cards offer no rewards, they often have promotional offers that will let you transfer the balance on your current credit card to the new one, which often allows you to carry that balance free of interest for the first six months (or a similar timeframe). There may be a fee somewhere in the neighborhood of 2-3 percent for transferring the balance, but if you have a lot of credit card debt, it may still be worth it to pay the balance transfer fee just to avoid paying an interest rate of 20 percent or more on your balance for six months. These cards may also have lower interest rates compared to higher-tiered credit cards even after your promotional interest-free period expires. Also in this category are "secured" cards: before the institution issues you a secured card, you must pay a security deposit that will be seized if you default on your payments. Thus, your spending on such a type of credit card is "secured" against your deposit. This can be a great way for complete beginners to build up their credit histories, since banks feel more comfortable with issuing a secured card to someone with a lower credit score. An example of a secured card is the Capital One Secured Mastercard (US). You should do your own research as to which specific options are available to you in your region.

Alternative Sources of Credit

If you find yourself in need of quick cash, you may be tempted to use a cash advance on your credit card or a payday loan. It is my opinion that you should never, under any circumstance short of immediate mortal danger, use either a cash advance or a payday loan. The typical interest rate for a cash advance on a credit card hovers at around 26 percent in Canada, and it is similar in the United States and other developed Western countries. The interest rate for payday loans can reach up to 50 percent! If you are in need of cash, it is worth looking into getting a line of credit instead. Yes, I know that a line of credit requires a decent credit score and some proof of the ability to repay, such as a stable steady income, and I know not everyone satisfies those conditions. But in my experience, many people don't look into this option or even know that it exists. The interest rate on a line of credit will typically be much lower than the interest on a credit card. A line of credit can also be secured against your house, which can further lower your interest rate. For example, a year after I entered university, I was offered a line of credit from my bank with a limit of $12,000 at an interest rate of about 4 percent. I was 19 years old at the time.

THINGS THAT I DON'T BUY (OR DON'T PAY FULL PRICE FOR)

I was lining up to order at McDonald's one day, at a time before the magic that is the self-ordering kiosk. The guy in front of me seemed to take his sweet time deciding what to get, and when he finally did order, I leaned in to listen. He ordered a Double Quarter Pounder BLT Combo, substituted the drink for a large strawberry milkshake, and substituted the fries with poutine (clearly this happened in Canada). When it came time to pay, his order was well over $20. I remember standing there, mouth open in shock. I was just going to order a couple of Junior Chickens, which would not add up to more than $5, and eat them at home, where I can pour myself a glass of cold water at the everyday low price of $0. I remember standing there wondering what this man did for a living that allowed him to spend so lavishly. As a first-year university student with no job and tens of thousands of dollars in debt, I could not fathom the riches one would have to accumulate to order whatever one wanted at McDonald's.

People often laugh at me and think I'm joking when I tell them that one of my dreams is to be able to go to McDonald's and order whatever I want without coupons. But I'm being totally serious. Perhaps the math would work out slightly differently depending on your location, but in Ontario, a typical combo meal at McDonald's can easily exceed $15 after you factor in the 13 percent sales tax. This may not seem like much at first, but consider how much food you are getting for that $15 combo—a burger, a medium box of french fries and a soda-fountain drink—you can probably make a similar meal at home for a third of the price or even less. Compound this fact with the frequency with which people purchase McDonald's, and you will quickly realize that it is one of the most expensive things people buy. You may think that steakhouses are expensive, and they are, but realistically, how often do you eat at a steakhouse each year? Probably significantly less than the times that you go for fast food. Although I ate my fair share of McDonald's when I was in university, I have to say that I have always either used coupons or ordered off the value menu, which is a brilliant strategy to mitigate most of the extra costs associated with eating fast food. Therefore, I classify fast food as one of the things that I have almost never paid full price for. I will now describe other items that I either do not pay full price for or refrain from buying in the first place.

Furniture

It always amazes me how much money people spend on furniture without blinking. Some people would drive to a gas station that's 10 minutes farther just to save a few cents per liter on fuel, then turn around and drop $3,000 on a new couch. Back in high school, I went to a friend's house once and was met with a sudden shout when I tried to put my backpack on his table. He quickly explained that his mum had recently spent over $1,000 on that fancy mahogany table, and everyone was forbidden to use it at all times. Sure enough, I took one look at the table, and there was absolutely nothing on it except for a decorative vase right in the middle. I asked my friend what the point of spending over $1,000 on something that no one could use was, and he explained to me that his mum was simply reserving the table for use on special occasions. Those special occasions came only a few times a year: big holidays such as Christmas and a few birthdays here and there. The rest of the time, the table remained completely empty and took up most of the common area in which it sat.

I know people want to splurge on furniture, especially when they move into a new home. But in the long run, making small sacrifices such as buying a simple table from **IKEA** at probably less than a fifth of the price of a fancy table (and investing the difference!) can make a huge difference to your financial future.

Clothes

There is absolutely no reason to pay full price on clothes unless you are a model or you need to dress up in a certain way to sustain your income. For the majority of us, keeping up with the latest fashion trends is a costly financial mistake. Female readers may feel that this one is targeted toward them, but in my experience, men can be just as impulsive (if not worse) when it comes to buying clothes. If you do an audit of your closet, you will most likely find that you do not wear the vast majority of the clothes you own; acquiring more clothes not only drains your wallet but also causes your closet to overflow. If you ever want to move, an overabundance of clothes adds to the complexity and effort required. So, donate whatever you do not wear or any clothes that no longer fit you—and if you really need to buy clothes, try to get them from the thrift shop.

Bank Fees

I am talking about that $2 fee you had to pay at the ATM last week when you were out of cash at the bar and were forced to use an ATM not affiliated with your bank. Or that time you forgot to keep enough money in your checking account when your rent was due and got hit with an overdraft fee. Or, quite simply, the random expenses such as monthly maintenance fees on a bank account that slowly eat away at your money. Part of this just comes down to self-discipline. Try not to forget any preauthorized withdraws for bills and try not to use ATMs that charge you a fee for withdrawals. The other part, though, comes down to picking the right bank account.

Let me ask you this: Out of all the bank accounts that were available to you, why did you choose your current bank account? If you're like most people, your answer would probably be something along the lines of, "I just went with the same bank as my parents," or, "It was just the first bank that I stumbled across." If this describes you, then, from a probability standpoint, you probably don't have the best bank account for your needs. Choosing a bank account this way is like walking into the first car dealership you see regardless of the brand and buying the first car you see. If you actually shop around for a bank account that minimizes unnecessary fees for features that you don't use, you have the potential to save a lot of money. Some examples that come to mind include Ally Bank (US), and Tangerine Bank (Canada).

Delivery Services and Ubers

So, it's late, and you're tired and hungry. It makes you feel good that you can summon food right to your doorstep by pressing a few buttons on your phone. Or perhaps you're trying to get somewhere, and though you're not in a hurry, you can save yourself a good 15 or 20 minutes of walking by calling an Uber. A typical food delivery costs about $3.50, and your options for using coupons on deliveries are often much more limited. Even if you catch a good promotion for delivered food, that extra delivery charge will eat into and may even cancel out any money you would have otherwise saved. For Ubers, there is a base fee for simply calling the Uber no matter how far you travel. I'm not saying that you need to cut these out completely—I'm just telling you to keep in mind how much these small conveniences cost you in the long term.

THINGS TO SPEND MONEY ON

Many people make the mistake of thinking that frugal living means you have to deprive yourself. Some of you may be already slightly annoyed at the fact that in the previous section, I made a whole list of things that I believe are wastes of money but that you may enjoy thoroughly. So, to pull a bit of reverse psychology on you, I'd like to make a list of things that you *should* spend money on. I argue that these things may actually help you achieve financial independence faster the more money you spend on them (to an extent and within reason, of course), and they are not even necessarily related to finance or investment.

Mattress

I know I mentioned that expensive furniture is a waste of money, but your mattress is an exception. We spend a third of our lives sleeping, so having a good night's sleep is essential to everything we do, regardless of our goals in life. Therefore, it is really not worth it to cheap out on a mattress that might cause you problems such as backaches or interrupted sleep, which negatively affect you the next day. Keep in mind that I do not mean that you should go ahead and drop $5,000 on a mattress right now; the point is to find a mattress that you are fully comfortable sleeping on and not be afraid to splurge a little if the one you prefer costs a bit more than other brands.

Insurance

For those living in the United States, this is especially relevant due to the fact that most people need to buy health insurance. It can be tempting to go without health insurance, especially if one is young and not expected to have any serious medical conditions. However, it is always a bad idea to go without health insurance no matter your age or how healthy you think you are. The whole idea of insurance is to cover you in case of an unexpected medical event; as the name suggests, such events cannot be predicted. A sudden medical bill has the potential to undo years of progress toward financial independence, and the risk is simply not worth it. For those living in countries where health care is covered, there are most likely still other forms of insurance that one needs to consider, such as home or car insurance. If you are a major or sole income earner in your family, it may be helpful to get life insurance to protect your family in case of your sudden and unexpected demise. Of course, no one wants to get into a car accident, have their home flooded, or (knock on wood) suddenly die. But it might just happen, so don't skimp out on protecting yourself and those you care about against these scenarios.

Electronics

This may be something of a personal preference, but it really bothers me when my electronics don't work or are slow. Many people attempt to save a few hundred dollars by buying a cheap smartphone, and maybe this works for them because they don't need any of the features available on new phones. However, for me, I believe it is still fantastic (and better) value to spend more than $1,000 on a very good smartphone, since this is something that I will use every day for years. The same is true for other electronics such as computers. If you have to wait just a few extra seconds for something to load each time you do anything on a computer or smartphone, that adds up to a lot of frustration and wasted potential productivity over the course of a few years. In the end, cheaping out on a smartphone or computer may save you, what, a few hundred dollars? That's just not worth it, in my opinion.

Software and Productivity Services

This category is very broad and can include things such as budgeting tools, VPNs, cloud storage or backup, password managers, antiviruses, or any type of software service that one may use for productivity purposes. Typically, these services and products do not cost more than $100 a year, and the benefits you receive out of them far exceed their costs, to me. If spending about $100 to $200 per year means you can keep track of your passwords safely or drastically reduce the chances of getting a computer virus, it seems like a no-brainer for me to be spending money on these.

EMERGENCY FUND

Before we dive into the world of investing, you must set aside a certain amount of money as your emergency fund. The actual amount can vary from person to person, but it is generally accepted that you should keep anywhere from three to six months' worth of all your expenses locked away in a high-interest savings account that earns at least 2 percent per year of interest (this guards the value of your money against inflation). This is the only money, besides what you need for your basic necessities and the occasional luxury, that you should *not* invest. In case of an emergency such as a sudden medical expense or being laid off from your job, an emergency fund buys you time to plan your next steps without immediate danger of eviction or starvation. I hope to be very clear in stating that this money, like its name suggests, should be used for true emergencies only. No, The Weeknd coming to your city for a concert is not an emergency that you can dip into this fund for. Chances are, you will encounter at least one true emergency at some point in your life. You cannot control when or what that will be, but you can still be prepared for it when it happens.

DOLLARS SPENT VS. DOLLARS EARNED

Before you spend any money, you should keep in mind that $1 you earn is not equal to $1 you spend, and I'm not even talking about inflation. I am talking about what I'm sure we all love the most in the world: taxes. In order for you to actually spend a dollar, you'd have to earn maybe $1.20 or $1.30, or some other amount greater than $1, depending on your income situation. In simpler terms, if you buy a $10 lunch in Ontario and pay a 13 percent sales tax on it—increasing the cost of the meal to $11.30—you may have to earn something like $12, $13, or even more, in turn, to spend that amount (due to income tax). Effectively, you spend much more than you realize each time you buy something. At this stage, simply recognizing this fact is key; the theme of taxes will come up again later in this book.

Part Three: Strategies, Tactics, and Pathways to FIRE

"You guys see this symbol? You know what it is?" The professor asked in a third-year undergraduate course about differential equations in financial mathematics. I shook my head; I've never seen that symbol before. "This is 'Eta'; it's a Greek letter. You guys are in math, you need to learn some Greek." We had run out of the more commonly used Greek letters—since all the other ones had already been taken up by other equations and theorems, the professor was forced to use a more obscure symbol. I'm sure that when I talk about investing, many of you feel the same way that I felt that day in my differential equations class. There's just so much information out there, and trying to take it all in is like trying to drink from a fire hose. Or, rather, trying to learn Greek. In university finance classes at least, I often felt that the professor spent 99 percent of their time talking about each detail of the mathematical derivations of a specific economic or financial theory, fussing over the equations; after the course was over, the professor would go, "Great, now you go do it in real life." And everyone in the class would think to themselves, "Gee, thanks." My goal in this section is to achieve a balance of giving a good explanation of the way these strategies work without being overly math heavy. At the same time, I want to provide enough specific guidance to help you start your own investing career.

SOME DEFINITIONS

Before we delve into the specifics, though, I want to formally define some vocabulary that will come up as we talk about investing.

Index

A quantitative indicator of some financial market that consists of a hypothetical portfolio of stocks, bonds, or other types of financial securities presumed to be representative of that market.

For example, a popular index is the Standard & Poor 500, more commonly known as the S&P 500, which is a hypothetical portfolio of stocks from five hundred of the biggest companies in the United States—this portfolio is used as an indicator of the performance of the US economy. Indices can exist for specific markets; for example, the Russell 2000 is an index that represents two thousand of the smallest US companies by market capitalization (more on this in a moment).

Index Fund or Exchange Traded Fund (ETF)

A fund comprising financial securities such as stocks, bonds, and other products that seeks to accurately represent an index and mirror the index's performance. Shares of these funds can be bought and sold the same way as regular stocks, and the fund gives the investor a way to invest into an index as a whole without having to assemble a properly weighted stock portfolio themselves. For example, there are many options investors can choose from if they wish to invest in the S&P 500 index; for example, the SPDR S&P500 ETF, more commonly known by its ticker symbol SPY, is an ETF that seeks to duplicate the performance of the S&P 500. By owning shares in SPY, an investor effectively owns a small portion of all the companies in S&P 500 (assuming properly adjusted weights) and can expect very similar returns to the S&P 500.

Market Capitalization

Market capitalization refers to the total dollar market value of a company's outstanding shares. Commonly referred to as "market cap," it is calculated by multiplying a company's outstanding shares by the current market price of one share. The purpose is to have a simple way of determining "how big" a company is in terms of dollar value.

Security (Financial)

A security is a financial instrument that holds some type of monetary value. This can be a stock, bond, stock option, or similar product. Securities are often described as being "fungible," which means that they can be exchanged with other securities of the exact same type. In other words, any given security is completely indistinguishable from another security of the exact same type.

Yield

Yield refers to the earnings generated and realized on an investment over a particular period of time, and is expressed in terms of percentages based on the invested amount. For example, if you invested $100 at the beginning of the year and received $110 in total at the end of the year (so, $10 in profits) then your yield for that year would be 10 percent.

Volatility

Volatility is a measure of the magnitude of the variation of returns for a given security or market index. In most cases, the higher the volatility, the higher the potential gain or loss the security would have, and thus the riskier the security would be.

Derivative (Financial)

A financial derivative is a security with a value dependent on the value of another asset (or a group of assets), called the "underlying asset." The derivative's price would thus "derive" from the underlying asset and fluctuate along with the price of the underlying asset itself.

Retail Investor

Retail investors are individuals who purchase securities for their own personal accounts rather than for organizations. This is in contrast to "institutional investors," who are almost always professionals in the finance industry who represent and trade in large volumes on behalf of investment banks, pensions, and other large funds or trusts.

INVESTING VS. GAMBLING: WHAT'S THE DIFFERENCE?

"Andy, in your opinion, what is the difference between investing and gambling?"

I was so shocked when my dad asked me this question that I could not produce a sound for a good 10 seconds. To me, that question is like asking a surgeon the difference between operating on a knife stuck in your leg and just, you know, leaving it in there because you can still kind of walk. It's like walking into a Ferrari dealership and asking the salesperson what exactly the difference between this Ferrari and a Toyota Corolla is. It's like... well, you get the point.

But then I thought about it, and I kind of realized where my dad was coming from. Having grown up in old-school communist China, where the stock market was seen as a symbol of the evils of capitalism, my dad saw very little opportunity during his youth to become educated in concepts such as investing. Even as Chinese economic policy started to loosen up and stocks eventually began to trade in China, there was still a lingering sentiment that buying stocks is a bit like going to the casino. My dad told me how, in the early days of the Chinese stock market before computers were around—an age when you had to physically go to the stock exchange to buy and sell stocks—clever traders would gauge the volatility of the market by looking at how many bicycles were parked in the area outside the exchange. A high number of bicycles indicated either some big news event or just general market exuberance or panic. People would buy and sell stocks of companies without doing any research on them, hoping to make a quick buck. Sometimes it actually worked; some people got rich overnight when the shares they owned of a company they barely knew the name of went up by thousands of percentage points. But sometimes, people would lose it all and even be driven to suicide. It really was Las Vegas out there. Although my dad worked in a bank, his work had little to do with investing. Though he would dabble in the stock market, judging from his question, I think deep down inside he still believed that investing is just another form of gambling.

I know that many of you reading this book who may not have grown up in old-school Communist China nonetheless believe that buying stocks is equivalent to gambling. I will attempt to justify why this belief is absolutely false and illogical.

Expected Value

First, we need to introduce a statistical concept known as "expected value." The expected value is *the predicted value of a variable, calculated as the sum of all possible values each multiplied by the probability of its occurrence.* Now, I know that's a mouthful, so let's look at an example.

Here in Ontario, there is a lottery called Lotto 649. For $3, you get a row of six numbers between 1 and 49, and if all six of your numbers match the winning numbers, you win the jackpot. The jackpot varies, but it usually hovers somewhere between $1 to $30 million. For the sake of argument, let's assume a large jackpot of $30 million. The odds of winning the jackpot are 1 in 13,983,816, according to the latest data in 2019 from the official Ontario Lotteries and Games website. This means your expected value is your potential gain ($30 million) multiplied by your chance of winning (1 in 13,983,816), minus the money you spent on the lottery ticket ($3), multiplied by your chance of losing (13,983,815 in 13,983,816). If you work out the math, you arrive at a final expected value of −0.854662632, which we will round down to just −$0.85. This means that on every ticket you purchase, the expected return on that ticket is a loss of 85 cents. In other words, if you bought enough tickets to ensure a win, you would still lose 85 cents for every $3 investment put in. In reality, the circumstances are even worse, since there is a chance that you will have to split the pot with other cowinners. Also, in certain lotteries, (especially those in the United States) lottery winners often end up receiving much less than the reported jackpot estimate due to taxes and other miscellaneous costs. Although there have been unusually large jackpots in the past that may seemingly yield a positive expected value (such as a historically large $64 million jackpot in March 2016), the aforementioned risk of splitting the pot renders this effectively still negative. This is not a coincidence. Lotteries have worked the math out beforehand such that the expected values on tickets always yield in their favor rather than in yours. Otherwise, if the expected value were truly positive, you could theoretically guarantee a win by buying every combination possible and pocketing the difference between what you spent on buying the tickets and your winnings, which would be a positive number instead. Casinos work in much the same way; the expected value of pretty much any game you can find in a casino is always positive toward the house and negative toward you.

I talk about expected values to illustrate the need for one to find positive-expected-value investments if one wishes to increase one's wealth, as well as how one cannot find those positive expected values by gambling. In contrast, investing in stocks is one potential area where positive expected values can be found.

Historical Evidence

I might have convinced you by now that throwing your entire life savings into the lottery or packing everything up and going to Vegas may not be the best idea. But why is the stock market a good place to park your money in, then? The reason is that the returns on the stock market as a whole over the long term have been proven to always yield a positive return, historically. Yes, I said "always." Keep in mind that I'm talking about over the course of 20 or 30 years, or even longer. Do you remember that financial crisis we had in 2008-9? If you had bought stocks at the peak of the market in 2007, when the S&P 500 was at about 1500 points, and you had held it until now without selling in a panic when the recession hit immediately after, you would've made modest gains, considering that the S&P 500 is at just over 2900 points at the time of this writing in August 2019. In other words, even if you had bought stocks at absolutely the worst time ever during the 2008–9 recession, over the course of 12 years you still would have made over a 90 percent total gain. In fact, looking further into the historical evidence, we can see there that there has never been a single 20-year holding period of the S&P 500 in which the returns have been negative. According to the records, the worst 20-year holding period of the S&P 500 occurred in the 20 years prior to May 1979, during which the annual return was only about 6.4 percent. In simpler terms, this means that even in the worst 20-year period ever, you still beat inflation by having your money invested in the market (assuming an average inflation rate of about 2 percent per year). That's pretty damn sexy, if you ask me. It is worthwhile to also keep in mind that this 20-year period occurred a rather long time ago, spanning the 1960s all the way into the late 1970s. Recent returns have been slightly higher, with the 20-year rolling average ending in 2016 yielding about 7.5 percent annually.

What Stocks Really Are

When you click the "buy" button on your stock brokerage account, what are you actually buying? No, I'm asking a serious question. A lot of people (including myself when I was 18) buy and sell stocks on a monthly or weekly basis without understanding what they truly are. Stocks used to be just pieces of paper before we did away with that, and now they're just numbers on a screen. Congratulations, you just spent hundreds or even thousands of dollars buying numbers on a screen. Try explaining that to your spouse when you get home.

But, of course, that's not what you are doing. Fundamentally, when you buy stocks, you are buying a business. You literally become a partial owner of that business. Now, granted, most of the time you own maybe a few shares out of a possible several billion, but brushing aside that fact for just one moment, pretend you are the owner of that business in full. Would you understand how your business generates its income and how much value it provides? Would you find that your business is well prepared for future changes, such as new technologies and societal shifts? Do you like the current direction of the business, or would you like to adjust its course? Your understanding of the business should be at the same level (or at least near the same level) as a hypothetical full owner's whether you own one share or a billion shares, because, in the end, you own a business. The amount of the business you own should really be just a small detail in comparison to the fact of your ownership. If you find that you cannot answer some of these aforementioned questions in a satisfactory way yet still made money on your stocks, this would have been by blind luck.

Dividends

Dividends are pieces of a company's profits that are paid out to the owners of the company. If you own stocks in a company, theoretically, you are entitled to a piece of the money that the company makes in proportion to how many shares you own. In reality, not all companies pay dividends. This is because the management of the company sometimes believes that it can reinvest the money back into growing the company further, which may be more beneficial for the shareholders in the business compared to just receiving the money directly. Sometimes, a company will not pay dividends simply because it is not yet profitable and has negative earnings. This scenario happens very often with newer tech companies, which often rely on funding from venture capitalists to continue their operations and may be a very long time away from being able to pay dividends. Note that it is completely up to the company's executive management to decide if or when to pay out dividends, and that the amount of dividends paid out can change depending on how well a company is doing. If a company does pay out dividends, these are often paid out every financial quarter (every three months). Whether a dividend of a stock is considered low or high is measured by its "dividend yield," which is the annual dividends paid out per share compared to the stock's share price. For example, if a stock pays out $5 per share annually and is currently trading at $100 per share, the dividend yield would be 5 percent. Note that dividend yield is inversely related to share price, meaning that yields go down as share prices increase, and vice versa.

In addition to yield, another important statistic to pay close attention to is a company's "payout ratio." The payout ratio represents the proportion of the company's profits that goes out to shareholders as dividends. For example, a payout ratio of 20 percent means that 20 percent of the company's profits is paid out in dividends. An investor would want this number to be as low as possible, since a high payout ratio indicates that there may not be room for the dividend to increase in the future, unless the earnings of the company itself increase dramatically, which is unlikely for most high-yield dividend stocks. Sometimes, a company will even borrow money to pay dividends with, which can cause the payout ratio to rise above 100 percent. This is typically a bad sign. Although it shows management's dedication to paying out dividends, this move is also unsustainable and makes the company highly vulnerable to an economic downturn. A mistake made by many beginner investors is what is often called "chasing the yield," in which an individual chooses to buy one dividend stock over another simply because the former has a higher yield. However, an investor's portfolio often performs much better by choosing a stock with a lower yield compared to its peers but also a lower and much more acceptable payout ratio. Investing in dividend stocks is a constant battle to find the right balance between yield and payout ratio.

INVESTING VS. TRADING, WHAT'S THE DIFFERENCE?

"You should see my friend's brother—he's a stock market investor."

When my mum said this to me in a rather concerned tone, I knew a lecture was coming.

"What about him?" I asked, hesitantly.

"His brain is absolutely fried from looking at computer and phone screens all day because he needs to keep up on the stock news! When you talk to him it's like he doesn't even hear you, he'd blank out as you're talking to him and just look straight into blank space or stare back at his phone, it's like he's retarded or someth—"

"Mum, don't use that word; it's not nice."

"Don't be like him! He's also gambling away not only his money but his mum's money. His mum is very old, you know, and she doesn't go out or spend any money and he just takes it all and puts it all on the stock market hoping to get rich overnight; that's why I don't invest!"

I was at a loss for words. I have tried on many occasions in the past to explain to my mum the difference between investing and trading, to no success. That said, I can totally understand the confusion. To the average person, trading and investing really do seem like the same thing. In both cases, you're putting your money into the stock market with the goal of making more money with your money. However, the difference lies within the timeframes of your investment and the level of risk you are willing to take. In essence, investing is the act of finding and understanding businesses at a fundamental level and leveraging that knowledge to make financial gains in the long term. The key phrase is "long term." By long term, I mean over the course of at least 5 years, and preferably 10 years or longer. Therefore, whenever I buy a stock, I do so because of three factors:

1. I understand the business to a degree that I feel comfortable putting my money into it.
2. I think the business is currently undervalued relative to its growth prospects.
3. I am comfortable with holding, and intend to hold, the stock for the long term (at least five years).

While I may not actually hold the stock for five years or longer (we will talk about conditions that may motivate an investor to sell a stock in a later chapter), that is my intention when I buy any given stock. Note that trading, as opposed to investing, is short-term in nature. Trading is the act of looking at technical indicators—such as candlestick charts, among many other tools—to try to make financial gains by holding financial securities for days, hours, sometimes even minutes or seconds. Unlike investing, trading does not involve the need to understand a business that one is buying or selling stocks of. The risks involved with trading are much higher, since volatility in the stock market tends to be much higher in the short term than in the long term. However, the potential gains in trading are also much higher than those in investing. In this sense, trading is much closer to gambling than investing is. When people hear about friends or family who have lost massive amounts of money "investing" in the stock market, they were most likely trading rather than actually investing. Of course, sometimes this works the other way, and we have all heard about that one guy who made it big overnight by dumping all his money into a penny stock. However, just like in the casinos, for every person who strikes it rich, many more lose a fortune. I am not advocating against trading per se; some people have a natural skill that allows them to consistently make high returns by trading stocks or other financial securities. I am saying that the vast majority of people who trade lose money. If you wish to become a successful trader, this book will not teach you that. I intend to teach you how to invest using principles that have been proven to consistently generate wealth over the long term.

Preferred Shares vs. Common Shares

I will not spend too much time in this book on details about specific "classes" of stocks that may carry different voting rights in a company. This is because the structure and classes of stocks can differ wildly from company to company, and it may be worthwhile for you to do your own research as to which class of stock you would like to purchase depending on whether you care about voting in shareholder meetings. However, there is a distinction between what is known as "preferred shares" and "common shares" that I think is useful to illustrate. Preferred shares are stocks of a company that carry higher priority in their claim to the company's dividends or asset distribution. This means that when dividends are declared, preferred shareholders get paid before common shareholders. In the event of bankruptcy, if there are assets left over after the company liquidates, preferred shareholders also take priority over common shareholders in the distribution of value from these assets (although bond holders have the highest priority; more on bonds later). The dividend amounts paid out to preferred shareholders are often explicitly stated, either as a set rate or one fixed to some benchmark interest rate like the London Interbank Offered Rate (LIBOR). However, preferred shareholders typically have no voting rights or, at most, limited voting rights compared to common shareholders. The advantage of preferred shares is that they allow investors to combine the beneficial features of debt (prioritized for dividend and bankruptcy payouts) and the beneficial features of equity (capital appreciation).

IPO Stocks

An Initial Public Offering (IPO) is what happens when a private company goes public and begins issuing shares to general investors for the first time. Usually, an IPO is something of a rite of passage for companies seeking to truly transform themselves into well-known empires. By selling shares to the public, companies have an opportunity to raise a massive amount of capital practically overnight. The usual process of an IPO involves a company enlisting the help of an investment banker, who tries to promote and sell shares to investment firms on behalf of the company seeking an IPO. This is called "underwriting," and often involves a "road show" in which the investment banker bounces between investment firms with the company's financial information and growth prospects in an effort to generate hype for the company. When the company's shares finally do begin trading on a public exchange, such as the New York Stock Exchange, small individual investors such as you and I finally get a chance to own part of the company. You may have heard about big companies that have recently had their IPOs and wondered to yourself if you should buy into their IPO stock. Although they are sometimes great opportunities, IPO stocks carry a significantly higher amount of risk compared to other stocks for the following reasons:

1. Information disparity and lack of historical data
2. Potential conflicts of interest
3. Second-mover disadvantage

First, and most glaring, IPO stocks have not proven themselves to be good businesses from an investment standpoint. Since the average investor does not have any historical information to base their investment decisions on, they suffer from a huge knowledge gap between themselves and the company's management team. Second, an IPO is, at its core, an opportunity for the owners of the company to cash out some of their stake in the company. Their intention is to sell their shares for as high a price as they can, which conflicts with your goal to buy shares at as low a price as possible, as an investor. The management can also pick the time period in which their IPO opens, so naturally, it picks a time when the market is favorable toward itself. Therefore, it is difficult for one to get a good deal on an IPO stock, as such events typically never happen during big market downturns, when other stocks go on sale. Third, by buying into an IPO stock as an individual investor, one is forced to buy the stock at a higher price than what big investment firms pay, since they get first priority to buy these shares. So, as an individual investor, you will always be at a price disadvantage if you decide to buy into an IPO, at least initially. For the aforementioned reasons, I would generally recommend against buying IPO stocks unless there is some overwhelming reason why you believe this business will grow and succeed in the long term.

THE TIME VALUE OF MONEY

The basis of the time value of money is that money now is worth more than money in the future. Imagine that I owed you $100 and I gave you two options. You can either have your money back now, or you can have it back a month from now. Which one would you choose? I imagine you'd choose to have your money now rather than later; the amount of money remains the same, so why not have it now? Alternatively, if I asked you whether you would like to have your $100 now or wait a month and get $105, which would you choose now? I'd imagine in this scenario, some people might be motivated to take the latter option, since if you're not in dire need and you could have an extra $5 if you were to just wait a month, why not? That $5 difference is what is known as "interest." In this scenario, if you were indifferent to taking $100 now or taking $105 in a month—meaning that those two options are entirely equivalent to you and that you would be just as happy with either—you've just set an interest rate. If you recall what we've already discussed about inflation, you'll note that inflation also exacerbates the fact that money now is worth more than money later. Recognizing the time value of money is crucial for doing estimates on a company's current value. When looking at a company's future earnings, those earnings must be "discounted" back to current amounts to get an accurate reading of their actual value. In essence, if $100 now is worth the same as $105 in a month, what if we are interested in what $500 in three months is worth now? If the interest rate is 5 percent per month, as it is in this scenario, you'd have to discount that $500 by 5 percent, three times; in other words, $500/(1.05)^3$, which gives you $431.92. Note that this is just an example and that in real life, interest rates are usually given in annual periods; they are also not usually this high unless the transaction is some type of payday loan or cash advance.

PRICE VS. VALUE

Let's say that you are deeply familiar with the price of a bottle of your favorite brand of laundry detergent. Suppose you've been buying that same brand of laundry detergent for years at the price of $10 a bottle. One day, you go to the store and find that, to your pleasant surprise, it is on sale for $5 a bottle. Even though you know that you still have plenty of detergent at home and that you're not in a hurry to buy more, you load up your shopping cart because you know that the sale will be over soon and the price will return to $10. And sure enough, you're right. The next time you go to the store, you find that not only did the price go back up, it has increased to $15 per bottle. You now feel that the detergent is overvalued, so you will refrain from buying any more. Even if you run out of your previous inventory, you think to yourself that if the price does not come back down to $10, you will switch to a different brand.

What I am trying to illustrate with this example is the difference between price and value. In this example, the price of the detergent fluctuates, but the value—as determined by you, the expert—is $10. I am sure we are all deeply aware of the value of one or two things, whether that's computer parts, cars or shoes. You can tell because these are the things that would make you go, "What?! That's way too much!" "Yeah, that's about right," or "Wow, that's cheap!" whenever someone else tells you what they paid for it. If stocks are one of those things, then you're well on your way to FIRE already. If they are not, then your goal is to try to apply to stocks the mentality you hypothetically would have applied to laundry detergent in this example. Say that you are invested in Stock XYZ at a cost of $100 per share. Consider, further, that the price of XYZ drops to $90 after a few days. Most beginner investors would at this point begin to panic—they may be tempted to sell the stock and cut their losses. However, this is the exact opposite mentality you should have. Say that you invested in XYZ because you believed that the value of the stock should be $110. If the stock price were to drop to $90, the most logical reaction should be to buy more stocks since you are now able to get them at a cheaper price. Conversely, if the price of the stock rises to $120, it is now overvalued in your mind, since you believe that the stock's value should be $110. Most beginner investors would be tempted to hold on to the stock, hoping that it would rise even more. However, the most logical reaction now would be to sell the stock, since by your own estimation you now know it is overvalued. The idea that one should buy a stock when it is going down and sell a stock when the price rises dramatically seems counterintuitive at first. Most people tend to do the exact opposite (and proceed to lose money as a result). When the stock price drops, they lose confidence and take a loss by selling. When the stock price rises quickly, they get greedy and hold on to it, missing out on gains when the stock falls back to its true value. This is the first mental obstacle you must overcome if you wish to have success in the stock market—your secret weapon is having confidence in your belief of what you think the true value of the stock is. I'm sure you must be asking the million-dollar question by now: "How do I know or find the true value of a stock?" We attempt to answer this question and go through some ways to evaluate a stock.

QUANTITATIVE MEASURES

We will now go through a few ratios and other quantitative measures to help you understand what a company is worth. Keep in mind that often, certain ratios are rather meaningless and do not provide much insight by themselves; they must be compared to the same ratios of other similar companies in the same or similar industries.

Earnings per Share (EPS)

The earnings per share figure is calculated by taking the total net income of a company (alternatively known as just "earnings" or "profits") less dividends paid on preferred shares, divided by the number of common shares outstanding:

$$Earnings\ per\ Share = \frac{End\ of\ Period\ Common\ Shares\ Outstanding}{Net\ Income - Preferred\ Dividends}$$

This is a measure of the profitability of a company. The higher the EPS, the more profitable the company is. Note that this value can also be negative if the company is not profitable. In essence, the EPS measures how much money the company makes (or loses) for each share of its stock. Note that there are other ways to calculate EPS, most notably what is known as the "diluted EPS," which measures EPS on the assumption that all possible shares that could be outstanding are issued. Note that a company's diluted EPS will always be smaller or equal to its basic EPS, as we have defined these terms.

Price to Earnings Ratio (P/E ratio)

The price to earnings ratio, sometimes also called the "price multiple" or "earnings multiple," is calculated by dividing the price per share by the EPS.

$$P/E = \frac{Price\ per\ Share}{Earnings\ Per\ Share}$$

This is one way to measure how expensive or cheap a stock is. The P/E ratio is a comparison of the current share price of the company relative to how much money the company makes. In essence, the P/E ratio describes how much money investors are willing to pay for the company's earnings on a particular day. A high P/E ratio denotes that investors believe most of the company's value lies in the future and that the company is expected to grow very quickly, living up to high expectations. This is very typical of high-tech companies. Conversely, a low P/E ratio implies that most of the company's value is in its current operations and that the company is not expected to grow very much. Companies that provide utilities and consumer staples tend to have low P/E ratios, since these industries typically do not experience massive growth. Note that looking at a single company's P/E ratio tends to be useless, since what is considered a high P/E ratio versus a low one is dependent on the P/E ratios of similar companies in the same industry. For example, a P/E ratio of 20 may be considered low for a high-tech company but extremely high for a utilities company. The average P/E ratio for the S&P 500 index as of late 2019 stands at about 22. If you find that a company has a lower P/E ratio compared to its peers in the same industry, this *may* be an indication that the company is undervalued, and vice versa.

Also note that if a company is not profitable, as is the case with many new tech startups that go public, the P/E ratio does not exist, since the company has no earnings. If so, the company may be harder to value, but we will discuss in detail other ways to value unprofitable companies without information on the P/E ratio.

Price to Earnings Growth Ratio (PEG Ratio)

This ratio is a modification of the P/E ratio that takes how much the company is expected to grow into account:

$$PEG = \frac{Price\ to\ Earnings\ Ratio}{Expected\ Growth\ Rate\ \%\ for\ Next\ 5\ Years}$$

Here is an example that illustrates how to use the PEG ratio. Consider two companies, X and Y. Suppose you evaluate these two companies for a potential investment, and that they are competitors in the same industry. Suppose further that you know the industry average P/E ratio should be about 20. Suppose that Company X has a P/E ratio of 18 and a five-year growth rate of 12 percent, and Company Y has a P/E ratio of 22 and a five-year growth rate of 20 percent. If you were to only consider the P/E ratio, you may conclude that Company X is undervalued and Company Y is overvalued. However, if we work out the PEG ratio for both using the formula above, we find that Company X and Company Y have PEG ratios of 1.5 and 1.1, respectively. So, Company Y actually has the lower PEG ratio, which may indicate that it is a better investment when taking projected growth into account.

Price to Sales Ratio (P/S Ratio)

This is a comparison of the price of a company's stock relative to its revenue. This ratio is useful for evaluating companies that are not profitable, since it does not care about earnings; it only considers the company's sales, usually on a trailing 12-month basis. It is calculated by the following equation:

$$P/S = \frac{Price\ per\ Share}{Sales\ per\ Share}$$

"Sales per Share" simply refers to the amount of total revenue (again, typically on a trailing 12-month basis) divided by the average number of shares outstanding. The higher the P/S ratio is, the stronger the business will seem, at least on the "top line." Although, once again, this ratio does not take into account the profitability of a company and should only be used by itself as a quick glance at a company.

Price to Book Ratio (P/B Ratio)

This is a measure of the price of a stock relative to the company's "book value" per share, which is the amount of assets owned by the company minus its liabilities, divided by the amount of shares outstanding. More concisely:

$$P/B = \frac{Price\ per\ Share}{Book\ Value\ per\ Share}$$

Note that a low P/B ratio can be an indication that a company is undervalued but can also mean that something is fundamentally wrong with the company. A low P/B ratio could be an indication of an ineffective management team or inefficiencies in a company's operations. Typically, the P/B ratio of a well-run company should be higher than 1. In times of financial distress or if the company facing the prospect of bankruptcy, it is possible for the P/B ratio to drop below 1.

Current Ratio

This is a comparison of a company's short-term assets against its short-term liabilities. Simply, the calculation is:

$$Current\ Ratio = \frac{Current\ Assets}{Current\ Liabilities}$$

In this case, short term, or "current," refers to assets that are liquid enough to be used or liabilities that are due within one year or less time. In essence, the current ratio measures a company's ability to meet its short-term debt obligations. If the current ratio is 1, then that means the company has exactly enough short-term assets to pay off all its short-term liabilities. Obviously, an investor would want the current ratio to be high, since a current ratio of less than 1 may be an indication that a company is not well-prepared to cover its liabilities; it may therefore run out of cash and face financial problems. That said, it is worth keeping in mind that if a current ratio is too high (compared to the company's peers in the industry), this may be an indication that management is not using the company's assets effectively.

Return on Asset (ROA) and Return on Equity (ROE)

These are generally regarded as measures of the effectiveness of the management team. The return on assets value is a comparison of a company's net profits divided by the average dollar amount of the total assets of a company, typically on a trailing 12-month basis.

$$Return\ on\ Assets = \frac{Net\ Income}{Average\ Total\ Assets}$$

Usually expressed as a percentage, ROA seeks to answer this question: "For every dollar of assets a company owns, what's the return on it?"

Similarly, ROE does a similar comparison but with net income versus shareholders' equity, which is defined as the total amount of assets minus the total amount of liabilities:

$$Return\ on\ Equity = \frac{Net\ Income}{Shareholders'Equity}$$

This measure is typically used to compare the company to other similar companies in the industry to evaluate its management's effectiveness. If the company has a higher ROE compared to its peers, this may be an indication of the company possessing a competitive advantage.

Other Ratios

Please note that this is far from an exhaustive list of all the possible ratios and quantitative measures that one can leverage when looking at a business. I have simply picked some that I have deemed important and applicable to most companies. Some ratios may be more important to some industries than others. For example, computing the inventory turnover ratio for a software company may be rather useless and will most likely not help you much in understanding the company better. It is up to individual investors to do their own due diligence to evaluate as much information as they can about a company, and also to pick out what kinds of statistics are important, before making an investment decision.

BALANCE SHEET ANALYSIS

A balance sheet is a summary of a company's assets, liabilities, and shareholders' equity at a given point in time, and it can be represented on an annual or quarterly basis. There are two other frequently used financial analysis metrics—namely, the income statement and the cash flow statement. For the sake of concision, we will just look at the balance sheet for now. The goal here is to develop the correct way of thinking when looking at a financial statement rather than to scrutinize every number or detail. Understanding a company's balance sheet is crucial in helping potential investors gauge the financial health of the company. We've already touched upon this topic slightly when we discussed a company's current ratio, but now I would like to talk a bit more about the balance sheet.

A Balance Sheet Example: Alphabet Inc.

We will use the example of the latest annual balance sheet from Alphabet Inc., which is Google's parent company. I will refer to the company as Google from now on for simplicity's sake, but keep in mind it is technically Alphabet Inc. I chose Google as an example simply because it is well-known enough that most people would be familiar with the company; the specific example does not impact the methodology used to evaluate a balance sheet. I've taken the following data from Morningstar.com, but this information is publicly available and can be found everywhere on the Internet.

USD in Million except per share data		2014-12	2015-12	2016-12	2017-12	2018-12
▼ Assets						
▼ Current assets						
► Cash		64,395	73,066	86,333	101,871	109,140
Receivables		9,383	11,556	14,137	18,336	20,838
Inventories		–	–	268	749	1,107
Deferred income taxes		1,322	–	–	–	–
Prepaid expenses		3,412	3,139	4,575	–	–
Other current assets		2,173	2,353	95	3,352	4,591
Total current assets		80,685	90,114	105,408	124,308	135,676
► Non-current assets		50,448	57,347	62,089	72,987	97,116
Total assets		131,133	147,461	167,497	197,295	232,792
▼ Liabilities and stockh...						
▼ Liabilities						
▼ Current liabilities						
Short-term debt		1,999	3,000	–	–	–
Capital leases		10	225	–	–	–
Accounts payable		1,715	1,931	2,041	3,137	4,378
Taxes payable		96	302	554	881	69
Accrued liabilities		6,386	7,097	9,086	11,278	13,796
Deferred revenues		752	788	1,099	1,432	1,784
Other current liabilit...		5,847	5,967	3,976	7,455	14,593
Total current liabilit...		16,805	19,310	16,756	24,183	34,620
► Non-current liabilitie...		9,828	7,820	11,705	20,610	20,544
Total liabilities		26,633	27,130	28,461	44,793	55,164
▼ Stockholders' equity						
Common stock		28,767	32,982	36,307	40,247	45,049
Retained earnings		75,706	89,223	105,131	113,247	134,885
Accumulated other comp...		27	(1,874)	(2,402)	(992)	(2,306)
Total stockholders' eq...		104,500	120,331	139,036	152,502	177,628
Total liabilities and ...		131,133	147,461	167,497	197,295	232,792

Figure 1: Consolidated (Annual) Balance Sheet for Alphabet Inc. 2014-18 Source: Morningstar.com

I will now quickly go through some of the things you should be looking out for in a balance sheet and some things that may not be immediately obvious at first. We should note that in the case of Google, all the numbers you see in figure 1 are given in units of millions of US dollars. This is done simply to make it easier to read by eliminating trailing zeroes, due to the gargantuan numbers we are dealing with when it comes to such a large company as Google.

First, we note that each column of numbers represents data from a single year, which is marked at the top. The balance sheet can also be viewed on a quarterly basis. Whether you look at annual or quarterly reports is up to you, but if you intend to hold a stock for a long-term investment (at least five years), the long-term trend from the annual balance-sheet reports should be a little more helpful.

From the labels, you will see that the company's "assets" and "liabilities" are split between "current" assets and "non-current" assets. Current assets are assets that can be quickly converted to cash in less than a year. The potential for an asset to be quickly converted into cash is called its "liquidity." The faster an asset can be converted to cash, the more "liquid" it is said to be. You can see some examples of current assets in the graphic above. Things such as inventory or accounts receivable are generally fairly liquid and can be put under current assents. Examples of noncurrent assets include things like "property, plants, and equipment." These are fairly illiquid; a manufacturing plant or specialized equipment typically cannot be quickly sold and turned into cash. Similarly, current liabilities are debts that need to be paid off in less than a year. These are sometimes also called "short-term" debts and include things such as payroll. A company's employees are unlikely to be willing to wait for more than a year to get their paychecks, so payroll liabilities tend to be both large and extremely short-term. Noncurrent liabilities include long-term borrowings such as issued long-term bonds or long-term leases. The shareholders' equity is simply the difference between total assets and total liabilities. In general, the relationship between assets, liabilities, and shareholders' equity is:

$$Assets = Liabilities + Shareholders'\ Equity$$

From the example, we can see that shareholders' equity include things such as common stock and retained earnings, which is money that the company has left over after paying their liabilities; the management can choose what to do with this money.

Grading Balance Sheets

Recall that the current ratio is the ratio of current assets to current liabilities. You get an idea now of why we want this ratio to be greater than 1. If the ratio is less than 1, this would imply that the company does not have enough assets that can be converted to cash within a year that would be necessary to pay off debts due within a year. A current ratio of below 1 is generally a dangerous position for a company to be in, unless the company has another way of getting cash in a short amount of time by somehow quickly raising more capital. To get a general idea of how to grade balance sheets, it may be helpful to develop a system with some benchmarks and put companies into different "buckets" based on what their balance sheets look like. I will now give an example. Keep in mind these are just my suggested criteria, so feel free to adjust this model based on your investment goals and risk tolerance.

Grade	Benchmark
A	Current ratio much larger than 1; little to no total debt.
B	Current ratio larger than 1 and more total assets than total liabilities.
C	Total assets versus total liabilities around even and current ratio at around 1.
D	More total debt/liabilities than assets and current ratio hovering at or below 1.
F	Current ratio significantly below 1; much more total liabilities compared to total assets.

Table 1: Sample Guidelines for Preliminary Balance Sheet Analysis

Based on this system of benchmarks, Google would rank as an "A" company as of late 2019 due to its particularly large cash reserves and relatively low amounts of debt compared to its assets. When thinking about long-term investments, it is generally a prudent practice to avoid low-ranked balance sheet companies such as those in the "D" or "F" grades, unless the investor has a very high risk tolerance and intends for the investment to be a purely speculative play.

VALUE VS. GROWTH INVESTING

There are only two ways to make money when you buy a stock. Either that stock will pay you dividends or the price of the stock appreciates (the amount of this appreciation is known as "capital gains"). In an ideal world, you will be able to find stocks that do both. However, in general, stocks that pay dividends tend to be more stable businesses that are expected to grow at a much slower pace compared to some other companies. The act of paying dividends out is, in essence, a management team's decision to return some of the value of the business back to the shareholders instead of reinvesting it into the business. Whether this is a good idea really depends on the company. Usually, with consumer staples or needs-based businesses, the investor would much rather have some of the value back in the form of dividends so that they may potentially invest that money in other companies with higher growth. These companies typically trade at relatively low P/E ratios and are known as "value" companies. In contrast, growth companies typically do not pay dividends, and shareholders are mostly still satisfied with this fact. This is because management believes that it would be more beneficial for profits to be reinvested back into the company than for them to be paid out to shareholders. These companies are expected to grow at a rapid pace (hence the name; they trade at relatively high P/E ratios and are typically high-tech companies. Therefore, stock investors typically fall into two camps when they buy stocks. Investors who are willing to forgo being paid dividends in hopes of achieving capital gains are known as "growth investors." It follows, then, that investors who are looking for a more stable source of income from dividends and willing to forgo more potential upside in stock price are known as "value investors." It is worth noting that there is more risk involved in growth investing versus value investing. However, in return for the extra risk, the potential upside from capital gains is also typically significantly higher than potential returns from dividends. Also, it is worth keeping in mind that these terms of "growth" or "value" investing are simply just rough guidelines and not mutually exclusive. Very few investors are pure-growth or pure-value investors; most tend to fall somewhere in between. However, it is worth determining whether your personality and investment style more closely match a growth or value approach, since this will heavily influence your tolerance for risk, your financial goals, and how to achieve these goals.

TRUST IN THE LEADERSHIP (OR NOT)

Suppose you find a company that looks good on paper. You do your research, and all the numbers check out. Does this automatically mean that the company is a good investment? A very important but often ignored aspect of investing in stocks is the quality and integrity of the management team. Call it the passion or drive for achieving the company's goals, the X factor, the chutzpah, or whatever you want—it's a combination of the company leadership's commitment to the business and their willingness to be honest with shareholders even if a negative event such as an earnings miss happens. Imagine that you were a shareholder of Apple Computers back in 1997, when the company brought Steve Jobs back to be the CEO in a desperate attempt to avoid bankruptcy. The fundamentals of Apple were horrible, and you would have had no reason to hold on to your shares unless you had a solid confidence that Jobs would be able to turn things around. Needless to say, you would have been rewarded handsomely if you had held on to Apple shares from 1997 until now. Of course, I am not advocating having blind faith in a company and just dumping all your money in; that would be a horrible way to invest. The point I want to get across is that as a shareholder, you need to be able to trust the management of the company the same way that Apple shareholders back in 1997 trusted Jobs; if you don't, perhaps reconsider investing in that company. Let me give you an example. In 2002, the CEO of Whole Foods, John Mackey, was asked about the challenges he foresaw for 2003. Mackey told it like it was in his letter to shareholders, stating, "We do not expect to sustain the excellent 10 percent comps we saw this year." Further in the letter, Mackey spoke about difficulties in integrating Harry's Stores, a chain that Whole Foods had acquired, into the larger Whole Foods network. Notice that Mackey did not try to hide the fact that sales were expected to slow down and was instead upfront about the challenges the company faced; in his letter, he avoided the use of buzzwords or too much jargon. In 2005, Whole Foods was valued at about $6.6 billion USD. In 2017, Whole Foods was acquired by Amazon for an estimated $13.7 billion USD.

In contrast with Whole Foods, another supermarket chain in the United States at the time was Albertsons. In a letter to shareholders in 2002, then CEO Larry Johnston stated that Albertsons was "in the midst of an exciting transformation" and frequently used phrases like "passion to win" and "solid business performance." Now, this would have been somewhat justified if the company truly had been performing in an exemplary manner. The trouble was, the earnings per share for this company had not grown at all in *10 years*, and its stock price had been flat for five years; the so-called "exciting transformation" was just a euphemism for a massive restructuring plan to sell off or close many stores in an effort to combat declining sales.

We see these patterns play out again and again in the business world. A more recent example: in 2019, the We Company attempted an IPO in an effort to raise money. No, "attempted" is not a typo. The company's business mainly revolved around their WeWork brand and service, which rents office spaces out, renovates them into nicer looking "coworking" spaces, then sublets these spaces to other companies. The company had originally intended to IPO at a valuation of about $47 billion USD in the summer of 2019. However, questions about the management of the company began to arise when it was revealed that then CEO Adam Neumann had sold $700 million USD worth of stock in the company shortly before the intended IPO. Now, it is not uncommon for insiders to sell stock once a company has reached a certain size; however, the sheer size of this sale was somewhat concerning to shareholders, to say the least. Furthermore, it was revealed in the IPO filing that Neumann himself owned many of the buildings that WeWork was renting out, which could be a massive conflict of interest. Last, investors were concerned about the company's deal with Neumann to license the use of the "We" trademark from Neumann for $5.9 million USD, who personally owns the trademark. These concerns about Neumann's conflicts of interest prompted him to step down as CEO in September 2019. The company tried to lower their valuation from $47 billion down to (supposedly) as low as $10 billion before deciding to cancel their IPO altogether. As of late 2019, it is reported that WeWork is expected to announce layoffs for about 2,000 of its employees, or about 16 percent of their workforce.

The ability to trust in the management of the company is both important and necessary if you wish to become a successful investor. The analogy that I always use is to imagine that you are about to board a plane. Would you rather have an experienced and skilled pilot with a low-tech old Boeing or an advanced fighter jet with a pilot asking you whether you have the "passion to win" while trying to sell you a box of vitamin supplements? Picking stocks comes down to a similar choice.

SHORT SELLING

You will often hear the terms "bull" and "bear" being tossed around in the investment world. In investment terms, being "bullish" means you believe that a certain investment will increase in price; imagine a bull thrusting its horns up into the air. Conversely, being "bearish" means you believe that the investment will go down in price; imagine a bear swatting its paws downward. Then, we have the terms "long" and "short," which denote your strategy on how you plan to make money depending on whether you are "bullish" or "bearish" about the market or a particular stock. Let us define what is meant by going "short" or going "long" on an investment. If you own and hold a stock with the intention of waiting until it goes up in price, then you are said to be "long" on the stock and making a bullish play—you are in the stock for the long term. If you make a bearish play, meaning that you are making a bet that the stock will decrease in price, you may short the stock, in which case you are said to be "going short." So how does one make money when a stock goes down? In other words, how can one short a stock? We will now detail a method called short selling.

Suppose your dad let you borrow his car for a couple months. Suppose that, without telling your dad, you decide to sell his car and pocket the cash. Now, you know that in a few months you will have to return the car to your dad, but you conclude that for whatever reason, you can buy the same car (or at least, one of the exact same age, make, and model) back in a few months for $10,000 less than what you sold it for. If you are correct, you do exactly that: you buy back the car to give back to your dad without him ever knowing that anything had happened, and you pocket the $10,000 difference. However, if your plan goes wrong—for example, if that particular car becomes super expensive within the span of those few months—you are forced to buy the car back at a much higher price and take a loss. This is in essence what short selling is, except instead of cars you do it with stocks. In summary, you borrow a stock that you don't own yourself and sell it. Since you sold a stock that you did not own (that you borrowed), you are now "short" of that stock. You will have to buy it back at a later date to return the stock back to whomever you had borrowed it from, hopefully at a lower price than what you had sold it for. This is called "covering." Your profit or loss is the difference of what you had sold it for initially and the price you paid to buy it back. When you go long on a stock, you are hopefully buying low and selling high. When you short a stock, you are essentially reversing the order; you are selling high *and then* buying low.

We will not spend too much time talking about short selling in this book due to the unfriendliness of short selling to beginner investors. This is primarily due to two reasons. First, the potential for loss associated with shorting a stock is theoretically unlimited. When one goes long on a stock (meaning, one buys the stock and holds it, hoping that it's price will increase), the most one can lose is 100 percent of the money invested (i.e., the stock price drops to zero). However, since short sellers make money when the stock drops and lose money when the stock rises, there is no theoretical maximum to the price a stock can reach. Therefore, if one shorts a stock and the stock skyrockets in price, the short seller stands to lose more than 100 percent of the money invested. Sometimes, when a stock is heavily shorted and becomes too heavily oversold as the price plummets, a small upward tick in price may turn into a massive upward spike due to an effect known as a "short squeeze," or a "panic buy." As the name suggests, the short investors begin to worry that the price will go up, since the stock had been heavily shorted, so they begin covering their shorts. As more and more shorts are covered, demand for the stock increases and drives its price up. As the price goes up, even more short investors panic and rush to cover. This begins a vicious cycle, as the situation for remaining shorts gets worse and worse, eventually turning into a full-blown panic as the price of the stock skyrockets. This is one reason why a stock might go up by double-digit percentage points in a day when no new news about the company has come out.

Second, the natural tendency of the stock market is to go up, as we discussed earlier in the section about historical trends of the stock market. So, unless one has a very specific reason to doubt the success of one particular company or some exclusive information about upcoming financial crises, generally, in the long term, the probabilities work against you by pushing the entire stock market up. I recommend against short selling for beginner investors. If one wishes to make a bearish play, we will talk about other methods for doing so later on in this book.

ACTIVE VS PASSIVE MANAGEMENT

Sometimes, when I ask people if they invest, people answer in the affirmative. Often, this gets me a bit excited, as I always love to hear what other people are so passionate about that they are willing to put their hard-earned money into. Perhaps it's some new tech startup that will change the world; perhaps it's the company that makes their favorite brand of makeup. I would think to myself, "Hey, I need someone who is familiar with the makeup industry," since it does not involve a product that I use very often but could represent a great investment opportunity under the right circumstances. Thus, I am always a bit disappointed when they reply with something like, "Oh, I just put my money into a mutual fund." I am not saying mutual funds are bad, but I've noticed a trend with most people I know who have bought mutual funds: those people often have absolutely no idea what exactly they've bought. I'm not sure if you, dear reader, have bought into (or know somebody who has bought into) a mutual fund, but if you have, then let me ask you this. First of all, how did you choose this particular fund over the others? Do you know the specific percentage breakdown of investments that composes this mutual fund? Do you know what the management fees associated with this mutual fund are and whether you are getting the best deal? Do you know the performance of this fund over, say, the past five years and whether it has outperformed or underperformed the market if benchmarked against, say, the S&P 500? I reckon most people will not be able to answer the aforementioned questions in a satisfactory way. In fact, my guess is most people filled out a questionnaire or had a 10-minute conversation with some salesperson at a bank, then picked a mutual fund from a menu like they were ordering a beer. To me, this is a somewhat illogical way to spend one's money. People feel guilty spending $8 on a fancy latte but won't even blink before dumping thousands of dollars into a mutual fund without knowing what they're buying. At least with the latte you can be relatively sure of what you are getting. If you didn't know me, and I came up to you on the street asking you to give me $500 every month for ten years and, in exchange, I promised to grow your money at a risk level that I deduced you could tolerate judging from our latest 10-minute conversation, would you say yes to this deal? I reckon that you wouldn't be too eager about this deal unless I wore a suit and a nametag that said I'm a "financial advisor." It sounds ridiculous, but this is exactly how a lot of people view investing: a black box that you throw money into; if it makes money then it makes money, never mind if it's significantly less money than the general market's rate of return. My point is, most people misunderstand mutual funds and invest in them for the wrong reasons.

To understand the philosophy behind mutual funds, we must first understand what is meant by "active" versus "passive" management. Active management is the act of using research and various other analytical tools to make constant adjustments to a portfolio of investments with the intent of achieving a higher rate of return compared to the market as a whole or some other benchmark. Active management often involves a fund manager (or sometimes a whole team of decision makers) who consistently makes decisions on what to buy or sell based on what he or she feels is the right move. For example, mutual funds are often actively managed; day-to-day adjustments to the portfolio are made at the whim of the fund manager or the fund managing team.

Passive management, on the other hand, is the opposite of active management. In passive management, a portfolio is constructed with the intention to mirror the performance of some index. It is called "passive" because the intention is that you leave the portfolio be and just let it go up or down according to the market. There may still be a fund manager, but their job is to make adjustments to the portfolio to better match the index instead of trying to outperform it. Passively managed portfolios often require smaller teams and are less costly to run since they are simply designed to track an index. For example, exchange traded funds (ETFs) fall into this category.

Criteria for Success

It is important to distinguish the goals of active versus passive management. In active management, the goal is to beat the market. So, let's say you wanted to run a mutual fund that is benchmarked against the S&P 500. Success for you would be that if the S&P 500 increased by 8 percent that year, your portfolio increased by more than 8 percent. Note that if the S&P 500 fell by, say, 3 percent that year and your portfolio fell by 2 percent, you would still be considered successful since you still beat the market. However, with passively managed portfolios, your criteria for success is how accurately you can track the market. Let's say you assembled a passively managed portfolio that tracks the S&P 500. If the S&P 500 falls by 2 percent and your portfolio rises by 3 percent, this is actually considered a failure due to the fact that it was not able to accurately mirror the movement of the index that you wanted to track. If the S&P 500 falls by 2 percent, success for you is watching your portfolio also fall by 2 percent.

Index Funds vs. Mutual Funds

All that being said, when should one choose to invest in a mutual fund over an index fund? Since mutual funds are actively managed, they often incur higher fees compared to passively managed index funds. The fees associated with investment funds are represented by what's called the "management expense ratio" (MER), sometimes just called the "expense ratio," in short. This is the cut that the management team takes for making adjustments to the fund. For example, if the MER on a portfolio is 3 percent, this means that management will take 3 percent of the value of the fund as their cut regardless of how well the portfolio performs. In other words, if the portfolio were to do nothing, it would still lose 3 percent as a fee to the management team. Furthermore, due to the opaqueness of what constitutes a mutual fund (many mutual funds do not disclose information about the specific companies they invest in, instead listing them under very broad categories such as "US Stocks" or "Canadian Stocks"), a mutual fund may invest your money into companies that go against your ethical values. This may include tobacco companies, weapons companies, or anything else that is socially controversial or that you may be against. If this is the case, you may inadvertently be supporting companies that hold values contradictory to your own. Of course, this may be an issue with broad-market index funds as well, but the problem is at least mitigated by the fact that ETFs often disclose the companies they're holding before you make the decision to buy into them.

As we mentioned before, passively managed portfolios tend to have much lower fees because the adjustments being made can largely be automated, since the fund is only trying to track an index. For example, one of the most well-known passive index funds is the Vanguard S&P 500 ETF ($VOO), which has a MER of just 0.03 percent. Compare this with the expense ratios of actively managed mutual funds, and one finds that they often range somewhere in the 3-5 percent range, which is a hundred-fold difference! Therefore, in order for one to justify buying a mutual fund over an index fund, the mutual fund must prove that it is able to consistently beat the market rate of return of a passively managed portfolio after the MER of the mutual fund has been taken into account. Empirically speaking, by looking at historical trends, most mutual funds have not been able to consistently outperform the market and often even underperform the market. For most people, who do not evaluate the performance of a mutual fund before buying it, this can be a costly mistake. If a mutual fund underperforms the market and the investor is charged a high MER on top of that, the investor stands to lose a lot of potential gains. To reiterate, the purpose of a mutual fund is to outperform the market by using active management. Very few mutual funds actually achieve this goal. According to a report by S & P Indices Versus Active (SPIVA), an organization specially created to keep track of the performance of actively managed funds over time, they found that in a period of fifteen years ending in 2018, a whopping 92.08 percent of actively managed funds had underperformed the S&P 500. If you are currently invested in an actively managed fund, you better be sure that you are invested in the 8 percent or so chunk of funds that outperform the market. Keep in mind that this high percentage of underperforming funds includes big hedge funds and trusts that most retail investors are not even eligible to buy into. Once you take this fact into account, it is conceivable, even likely, that there does not exist even a single actively managed fund that the retail investor can buy into that outperforms the market. Unfortunately, if you have bought into a mutual fund from your bank, chances are that you would have made way more money if you had just bought into an index fund.

Passive Management vs. Picking Stocks

Maybe by now I've convinced you to ditch your mutual fund in favor of an index fund. Passive management is always better than active management, and that's the end of the story, right? What if I told you the answer is "no"? What if there is an even better way to invest your money? I'm talking about picking individual stocks yourself. Keep in mind that this falls under "active management," as you are making decisions about which stocks to buy and what proportion each stock makes up in your portfolio. Also keep in mind this involves you doing actual work researching and studying investing instead of just throwing your money at someone to do it for you or putting it in an index fund.

Now, you may be scratching your head at what seems like a contradiction: I'm telling you that you can beat the market when I'd just told you in the same breath how over 90 percent of professional fund managers fail at the same task. However, we will soon talk about the advantages that small retail investors have over hedge fund managers and how that can be leveraged to help you beat the market.

For now, just try to put a little more trust in yourself. I believe with some discipline and a bit of hard work, almost anyone can pick stocks and not only grow their wealth a lot more quickly but also get to be a part of companies and causes that you believe in and are passionate about. Besides, if you want to retire early, you definitely need to do at least a little better than the market average. These are your own hard-earned dollars after all. You should choose how to invest them.

REAL ESTATE INVESTING

We will only briefly touch upon real estate investing in this book, since the barriers to entering the world of real estate can be rather high for beginners compared to those of the stock market. However, keep in mind that there exists a plethora of books and courses available on this topic, if this is the route of investment that you choose. In this section, I will briefly explain the benefits of real estate investing and how it may fit into your strategy of achieving FIRE—but first, let's look at the concept of financial leverage to figure out how.

Financial Leverage

The process of using debt to invest and generate a greater amount of returns.

Think of financial leverage the same way you would think of leveraging something in the regular sense. Moving a big rock is easier if you were to stick a long bar of metal underneath it rather than use a shorter bar or move it with brute force. Financial leverage works the same way. If you invest borrowed money, you stand to gain bigger returns if you are proven to be correct. Of course, the more financial leverage you have, the riskier your investment becomes. If you are wrong, and the investment turns sour, you'd not only have to eat the losses on it but also pay back the money you borrowed on top of that. That being said, real estate investment is one great way to strike a happy medium between maximizing your potential returns and limiting your risk when you use financial leverage.

Leverage in Real Estate

People rarely buy houses in cash due to the high price of houses; as a result, banks usually only require a 20 percent down payment on a house. Provided that an applicant has a high and stable enough income as well as a satisfactory credit score, banks are usually willing to loan out the remaining 80 percent as a mortgage. Furthermore, since mortgages are secured against the properties that you use them for, they are one of the best ways to borrow money because of their much lower interest rates compared to personal loans or any other unsecured loans. At the time of this writing in 2019, the average five-year fixed-mortgage interest rate in Canada sits at about 3 percent, which will of course be significantly lower than any other type of loan. Mortgages represent a tremendous amount of financial leverage accessible to most people. Every dollar you have represents five dollars in the real estate world. This means that having $200,000 will effectively allow you to buy a million-dollar house. In some cases, and under special circumstances, a bank may even offer to lower your required down payment to 5 percent if you intend to live in the house that you buy as a primary residence for a prespecified number of years. This represents a 20X leverage, an amount that is pretty much unheard of in the stock market unless an investor is willing to make an extremely risky play—provided one can even get access to that kind of leverage in the first place.

House Hacking and Rent Hacking

Once you've effectively utilized the extreme leverage that's available to you in the form of a mortgage, you may want to start increasing your net worth through a process called house hacking. House hacking is when you buy a property with multiple rooms or units and rent out the rooms or units you are not living in. If you do this correctly, the rent money that you bring in from the other rooms should be enough to not only cover your mortgage payment but also leave a little bit extra on top. The extra money you have left over from receiving your rent and after you've made your mortgage payment is called the "margin of safety," or your "positive cash flow." If you manage to achieve this state of positive cash flow, you will not only be building up equity by paying down more and more of your mortgage each month but also have more capital to further invest in stocks or real estate.

An alternative version of house hacking is rent hacking. This is basically the same idea, but instead of buying a property, you sign a lease for a multiunit property and sublet the extra units. Rent hacking is easier to get started with since you do not have to contribute the large sum of money needed for a down payment. Although you do not build up any equity in real estate by rent hacking, you can drastically lower or even eliminate your living costs with this method if done correctly.

Cash Out Refinancing

A neat trick can be done in real estate investing that can help you build your net worth up very quickly, which I will illustrate with an example. Say you wanted to buy a house worth $200,000 with a 20 percent down payment—which would be $40,000—and you take out the remaining $160,000 as a mortgage. You then spend a further $30,000 renovating the house. Note that at this point, you have contributed a total of $70,000 to the property (your down payment plus what you spent to renovate it). Now, let's assume that after you finish your renovations, the value of the property appreciates to $280,000. You can then ask the bank for the same 80 percent loan on what the property is worth now, which works out to be $224,000. You then use this $224,000 to pay off your original loan of $160,000, and you are left with $64,000 in cash. Note that since you contributed $70,000 to the property and got $64,000 back, you effectively only have $6,000 tied up in the property while maintaining full ownership. You may use the $64,000 in cash that you now have to invest in more real estate and repeat this process. This process is called a "cash out refinance" and is frequently used by professional real estate investors. Note that since you are paying the mortgage on a higher loan amount, a cash out refinance will cause your monthly mortgage payment to increase. However, this small caveat is usually worth it due to the amount of investment opportunity that a cash out refinance brings.

Alternatively, another form of refinancing is known simply as a mortgage refinance: when interest rates fall, the borrower has an opportunity to negotiate a lower interest rate on their mortgage with the bank. Due to the large absolute amount of money borrowed when it comes to mortgages, oftentimes even tenths or hundredths of percentage points of difference in interest can translate into large amounts over the course of the lifetime of the mortgage.

REITs

REIT stands for "Real Estate Investment Trust" and refers to a company that owns, and in most cases operates, income-producing real estate holdings. Investors can buy into a REIT the same way they do stocks and ETFs. REITs allow investors to gain exposure to real estate without having to commit hundreds of thousands of dollars into buying properties themselves or worry about managing a property. REITs generally pay regular dividends out and can be a great way for small investors who have limited capital to gain access to a stable source of dividend income. However, a disadvantage of REITs is that they often offer very little capital appreciation compared to stocks and sometimes carry higher management fees compared to stock market index funds. When evaluating REITs, investors should approach them in much the same way as any other investment and keep some goals in mind as to what they want to achieve with the investment. In this case, REITs are generally geared more toward value and dividend investors than growth investors.

GOLD AND CRYPTOCURRENCIES

Many people misunderstand the role that gold and cryptocurrencies play in our economy and, as a result, mistakenly believe that they are "investing" when they buy gold or Bitcoin. However, as you will soon see, gold and cryptocurrencies do not fit the criteria of a good investment, and one should never buy gold or cryptocurrencies with the intention of holding these as investments.

Hedge

A hedge is a financial instrument or security used to reduce the risk of adverse price movements in a portfolio or asset.

Intrinsic Value

Intrinsic value refers to the value of a company, stock, currency, or product determined through fundamental analysis without reference to its market value.

By this definition, both gold and cryptocurrencies are hedges due to their lack of intrinsic value. For example, if you were to buy a bag of rice, it would have at least some intrinsic value, since you can eat it. If, after buying a large truckload of rice (with the intention of reselling it) you discover that the market price for rice has plummeted for whatever reason, the rice would still be worth something, since people need to eat. In the worst case, say, you're unable to sell the rice even at a loss for some reason, you can still eat it yourself; it will therefore still have some value to you. If you have bought shares of a publicly traded company—and provided you trust that its reported numbers are accurate—you can look at the company's financial statements and determine with some degree of confidence how much you believe the company is worth. (A caveat: gold does indeed have *some* intrinsic value due to its applications in electrical circuits for its conductive properties. However, for the sake of this argument, this intrinsic value is negligible due to the high valuation of gold for reasons that are completely unrelated to its use in electrical circuits.) In the case of gold, societies have used it as a store of value for centuries. In a market downturn, when people lose faith in the currency issued by their own government, many inevitably turn to gold, which has traditionally been acknowledged as valuable, thus driving up its price. Therefore, owning gold can be a great way to hedge against the risk of a market downturn if you believe that a recession is about to occur. Furthermore, due to the fact that gold prices are heavily influenced by emotions of fear and greed, large gains can potentially be made by trading gold. However, as we previously discussed, trading is not the same as investing. Gold does not "generate" money the same way owning a business (owning shares of a company), lending money out and collecting interest on the loan (bonds), or owning real estate do. If we look at the empirical evidence of the long-term performance of gold against a benchmark such as the S&P 500, we can see that between 1978 and 2018 (a 40-year span), the S&P 500 made a return of 630 percent, adjusted for inflation. If we look at the inflation-adjusted return of gold during that same 40-year period, we find that the return sits at only about 45 percent. There are costs and risks associated with the storage of physical gold, as it is heavy and needs to be secured against theft. If you keep physical gold at your house, you are unnecessarily exposing your wealth to robbery or natural disasters such as floods, fire, or hurricanes. If you decide to store gold in a safety deposit box at a bank, there will be costs associated with maintaining the box with the bank.

Furthermore, since we are in the business of long-term thinking, if we take an extreme-long-term view on gold, humanity may feasibly develop advanced enough technology to mine asteroids for precious metals such as gold in the next 100 years. If such a technology were to be developed, it may begin to erode the "store of value" appeal of gold, as gold will no longer be scarce.

I will not go into detail right now about the specific technologies that power cryptocurrencies, but at its core, the idea of cryptocurrencies is to create a currency that is wholly digitally based and, in the case of popular cryptocurrencies like Bitcoin, completely decentralized. Cryptocurrencies are also hedges and stores of value in much the same way as gold. Thus, cryptocurrencies suffer from the same problems as gold from an investment standpoint. One cannot "invest" in a currency such as Bitcoin for the same reason that one cannot invest in a traditional currency such as the Yen or the Euro. Like gold, Bitcoin does not generate cash flows, and its price fluctuations can be attributed solely to market sentiment. However, the cryptocurrencies are arguably worse stores of value than gold due to their volatility. If you had bought Bitcoin during the big run-up in its price in late 2017, when Bitcoin hit its peak on December 17, you would have paid $19,783.06 USD for one Bitcoin. A few months later in February of 2018, the price fell to just $6,300 for one Bitcoin. That's about a 68 percent loss in a little over two months! If your intention had been to use Bitcoin as a store of value, this would have proven a horrible idea.

ADVANTAGES OF SMALL INVESTORS

When you first start your journey in the wonderful world of investing, you may be intimidated by the fact that many seasoned professional investors are dealing with much larger amounts of money than you. Big hedge funds and investment firms make millions of dollars' worth of transactions per day, so naturally you may believe that they are at an advantage over small individual investors such as yourself. As you will soon see, however, small investors have many advantages over large investment funds in several key aspects.

Mobility

In 1999, when shares of the Coca Cola Company (KO) hit an all-time high, many investors believed (rightly) that the stock was overvalued. Warren Buffett, who held a significant number of shares in Coca Cola, was asked later, after the price of the shares had inevitably plummeted, whether he knew at the time that the shares were overvalued. Buffett replied that he did in fact know this. Of course he did; one does not simply become known as the "Oracle of Omaha" for no reason. The natural follow-up question then was, Why didn't he sell the shares? Buffett replied that he was no longer "nimble." Essentially, this means that if he had begun selling the shares, he would have single-handedly caused the price of the shares to collapse due to the sheer number of shares that he owned. The reverse would also be true for any big company or investor seeking to buy shares of a company. If a big investment firm such as Warren Buffett's company Berkshire Hathaway were to buy shares of a smaller firm, it would be conceivable—even likely—that the act of buying the shares itself would single-handedly drive the price of the shares up, which would cause the return on the investment to plummet. As small individual investors, our singular decisions to buy and sell shares of a company will not have any perceivable impact on the share price, and we can get in and out of a position extremely quickly, literally in a matter of milliseconds. This quality is often referred to as "nimbleness," or "agility," and this is not available to big investors.

Performance Pressure

Many big investment firms often have very strict criteria as to the kinds of companies they can invest in. The companies that they are allowed to invest in generally tend to be large-cap companies. This is because although large-cap companies tend to offer smaller rates of growth compared to smaller cap companies, they are less risky in general, and investment firms can invest a larger amount of money into them. As a result, very often, big investment firms will miss out on big growth opportunities offered by smaller up-and-coming companies simply because these companies do not fit certain investment criteria. Remember that investment firms and hedge funds often invest on behalf of clients; most clients will inevitably panic if they see their portfolios decrease by double-digit percentage points. Investment managers are under heavy performance pressure to keep their clients happy, even if this involves passing up huge growth opportunities, simply because they can't afford to take the risk on some smaller companies. Fund managers also are often incentivized to be fully invested at all times, since it is often hard to explain to a boss or a client why sitting on a large amount of cash for long periods of time is a good idea. As a small individual investor, you have the luxury of not being beholden to any clients who demand a set rate of return; you may sit on cash for as long as you want while awaiting a good opportunity, and you may choose whatever stock you want to invest in.

ESG Investing

ESG stands for "environmental, social, and governance," and the concept of ESG investing is picking companies that you believe are ethical and sustainable. Examples of topics in ESG include social and environmental issues such as climate change, animal welfare, human rights, worker compensation, and so on. If you were the fund manager of a big investment firm, you may be forced to invest in companies that go against your own personal beliefs. As a small investor, you have the opportunity to invest in companies that align with your ethical values.

BONDS AND THE YIELD CURVE

Bonds are debt instruments that can be either secured against real assets such as mortgages or unsecured. The borrower of the debt, in this case called the "bond issuer," agrees to pay the bond holder (the lender) an interest rate that is agreed ahead of time—this is called a "coupon" rate. Bonds also carry a face value and a maturity date. The maturity date is how long the holder will have to wait before the bond becomes due and the holder receives the face value of the bond. The face value, in turn, is the final payment after the bond matures, and it must be discounted back to its current value due to the time value of money. Until maturity day comes, the bond will continue to pay the holder interest payments known as "coupons" (usually on a semiannual basis) according to the coupon rate. This coupon rate will determine the price of the bond, which can be influenced by the general market interest rate. If the coupon rate is higher than the market interest rate, then the bond will trade at a price above its face value, since the payments one would get from it would be higher than what the investor would get from the prevailing market rate. Such bonds are called "premium bonds." Conversely, if the coupon rate is below the prevailing market rate, the price of the bond will be lower than its face value. These are called "discount bonds." In a scenario where the coupon rate matches the prevailing interest rate, the bond is said to be a "par bond," or "trading at par." Since the size of the coupon payments is known beforehand, the investor knows precisely how much interest income to expect over the life of the bond. Thus, bonds and other related debt instruments are known as "fixed-income securities." There are two main types of bonds: government bonds and corporate bonds. As its name suggests, a government bond is issued by the government, and these bonds usually carry the least amount of risk (at least if you are in a country such as the US, where the government never defaults on its bond payments). The gold standard of bonds is the US Treasury Bond, which are considered risk free. This is because even in the unlikely scenario that the US Treasury runs out of money to make its coupon payments with, it can simply print more money to pay off its debts. Although in practice this would indeed lead to inflation, the negative effects of defaulting on US Treasury Bond payments would be much more disastrous than the inflation that would be caused by printing more money. Needless to say, printing more money is not a luxury that is afforded to corporations, and corporations tend to carry a higher risk of default than the government to begin with. Thus, to compensate for the added risk, the coupon on corporate bonds would be higher than that on government bonds. We will not go into detail right now about the math used to calculate the price of a bond; rather, let's aim to get an understanding of the concept of bonds in general here, most notably through discussing the "yield curve" and how it relates to the entire financial market.

The "yield" of a bond can simply be thought of as one's annual return on an investment expressed as a percentage. If you were to invest $100 and receive $10 a year later, your yield would be 10 percent. When people talk about "the yield curve," they are often referring to the comparison between the yields of a 2-year US Treasury Bond versus a 10-year US Treasury Bond. Normally, when people invest their money for a longer period of time, say 10 years as opposed to 2 years, they will expect a higher yield on the longer-term 10-year bond, since they would be required to tie their money up for a longer period of time. This effect becomes more exacerbated the further away the maturity date is, creating a line that curves upward. However, in times of fear and panic, such as if investors believe a major recession or economic slowdown is imminent, the demand for longer-term bonds will spike, as investors seek a safe place to stash their money. This causes an increase in price for longer-term bonds. We should note here that the price of a bond and the yield of a bond are inversely related. This means that if the price on a bond goes up, the bond's yield will go down, and vice versa. Intuitively, if the price on a bond increases and your return on the bond stays the same (since the coupons are fixed), that means you would have to spend more money on getting that same return, thus decreasing your yield. Imagine that for the same $10 return in the previous example you invested $125 instead of $100; your yield on the investment would drop to 8 percent. As prices on long-term bonds increase and their yields continuously fall, the yield curve "flattens." If this pattern continues, the yield on long-term bonds, such as the 10-year Treasury Bond, can actually drop below the yield on a 2-year Treasury Bond. This is known as a yield curve "inversion," and it is often used as a sign of an incoming recession. Of course, there exists more than one yield curve. The 2- versus 10-year Treasury curve is only one such indicator of its kind.

STOCK OPTIONS

Imagine that you're at the electronics store and you saw a great deal on that new laptop that you want. The regular price was $1,200, but now it's on sale for $1,000. You excitedly ask the salesperson to ring you up. However, you are soon disappointed to hear that the store has sold out of that particular model and that a new shipment will not come in until next week, long after the sale is over. If you are lucky, though, the store may issue you a rain check, which allows you to purchase the item for the sale price when it's back in stock, even if the sale is over. The salesperson issuing you the rain check warns you that if you wish to use it, you must redeem it within a month, or it will expire. You happily agree, take the rain check, and leave the store. You've just created, in effect, a *call option*.

An option is the right but not the obligation to buy or sell an asset at a predetermined price on or before a predetermined date. For example, going back to the rain check, you are not obligated to redeem the rain check. If you find another laptop you like as soon as you walk out of the store, you may opt to never redeem the rain check, and things would be fine. The act of redeeming an option is called "exercising" an option. The predetermined price—in this case, $1,000—is called the "strike price." And the date you must exercise your option by—in this case, a month from now—is called the "expiration date." A call option allows you to buy a security or some other asset at a predetermined price. The security or asset that it is linked to is called the "underlying asset"; in this case, the underlying asset to the rain check is the laptop. As you can see, the value of the call option depends on the value of the underlying asset. This is why options are known as "financial derivatives," since the value of the option "derives" from the value of the underlying asset. If the value of the laptop were to increase to $1,500, your rain check would also increase in value. More precisely, it is worth the difference between the strike price and the price of the underlying asset. If the price of the laptop drops to $900, your rain check would be worthless, since it would cost you more to exercise the option and buy the laptop than just buying the laptop at market price. Take this example and apply it to stocks—it is the exact same idea. Your payoff from a call option can be represented by the equation:

$$Max[0, Price\ of\ Underlying - Strike\ Price]$$

As you can see, holding a call option is a bullish play. This means that you will make money if the stock goes up in value and lose money if it goes down.

The opposite of a call option is called a "put option." A put option is the right but not the obligation to sell a security at a predetermined price on or before a predetermined date. For example, Company XYZ is trading at $100 per share, and you own a put option with a strike price of $90, at expiry; if XYZ trades at $75, you can buy a share of XYZ on the market for $75, exercise your option to sell XYZ at $90, and pocket the difference of $15. If the price of XYZ remains above your strike price of $90 at the expiry date of your put option, it will expire worthless. In particular, the payoff equation for a put option is the following:

$$Max[0, Strike\ Price - Price\ of\ Underlying]$$

Holding a put option is a bearish play. This means that you will make money if the stock goes down in price and lose money if the price goes up. Holding put options can be a good alternative to shorting stocks if you believe that a stock will decrease in price in the future. This is because your potential losses when holding options are capped at 100 percent of your investment, which is not the case when shorting stocks, as your losses are theoretically unlimited when shorting.

Although many people trade options, they are mostly used as hedges in a larger investment strategy to limit risk. Buying or writing options without the intention of using them as hedges can be very risky and is inherently a short-term play, as options have expiration dates. If one chooses to write an option (meaning, to sell an option) without owning the underlying stock (or the cash needed to buy the underlying stock in the case of a put option exercise), then such a play is called a "naked" play.

Note that options are typically sold in "contracts," where each contract contains 100 options. In other words, each options contract controls 100 shares of the underlying stock, and investors are required to buy and sell (or exercise) in increments of 100 options.

An Example of Using Options as a Hedge: The Covered Call

We will go through just one of the myriad strategies and payout functions one can construct using options. One of the simplest options strategies is called the covered call, and it is used to mitigate the risk of price downturn on a stock that you own. The idea of a covered call is to write a call option against a stock that you own. Remember that buying a call option is bullish play in itself. Thus, the act of writing a call is a bearish play in itself, meaning that you profit if the stock price decreases. However, if you combine writing a call on a stock while holding the stock, this means that if the stock price goes down, you will make back some of the money that you had lost from capital depreciation on your stock due to the call options you had written expiring worthless and therefore never getting exercised. If the stock price goes up (above the strike price of the written call options), then the call options will be exercised; you will be forced to sell your stocks at the strike price and give up any gains you would have made on capital appreciation beyond the strike price of the call options you had written. In other words, this strategy allows you to use call options to protect you from a downturn in the stock price at the cost of capping your gains on the stock if the stock price goes up. Let's go through an example from chapter 2 of *Options as a Strategic Investment* by Lawrence G. McMillan.

Suppose you buy 100 shares of XYZ common stock, currently trading at a price of $48 per share. Suppose that you are mildly bullish on the stock (meaning that you believe that the price will increase mildly in the near term), but you want to protect yourself from a potential price decrease. To do this, you write some call options with a strike price of $50. Suppose that you receive $300 from the sale of these call options.

If, by the expiry of the call options, XYZ stock is still trading at below $50, the calls will expire worthless, you can pocket the $300, and you still own the stocks.

If, by the expiry of the call options, XYZ stock is trading at $60, the options will be exercised and the stocks called away at a price of $50 per share. Since you had bought the stocks at $48 per share and sold them at $50, you will have made $2 per share—$200 of profit in total, since you had 100 shares. Further, you still made $300 from the sale of the options. So, your total profit on the entire trade is $500. Note that although you still profited, if you did not write the call options, you would have been able to sell your stocks in XYZ at the market price of

$60 per share, which would net you a profit of $12 per share, or $1,200 for 100 shares. Therefore, you have protected yourself from a decrease in stock price by giving up potential capital gains and capping your total potential profits.

Note that alternatively, instead of allowing your stocks to be called away, you may choose to cover your call-option writes by paying the intrinsic value on the calls, which is the difference between the market price of the underlying stock and the strike price of the option. For example, in the scenario where the stock price is $60, you may release yourself of the obligation to sell the stock at $50 by covering the calls that you had written at the cost of $1,000 ([Stock Price − Strike Price]*100 shares). Keep in mind that you would still make $300 from the initial sale of the calls, so your total loss from this trade will be $700. However, since you've relieved yourself of the obligation to sell XYZ at $50 by buying the calls back, you now hold 100 shares of XYZ that you can sell at $60—an unrealized gain of $1,200 in total. Subtracting the $700 you lost from the previous transaction of covering your calls, your total unrealized profits is $500: the exact same as in the previous scenario. Therefore, either letting the calls be exercised and your stocks be called away or buying the calls back at a loss yields the exact same returns.

Formally, we can use these formulas to quickly calculate both the maximum potential profit and the breakeven point for your calls:

$$Maximum\ Profit\ Potential = Strike\ Price - Stock\ Price + Call\ Price$$

$$Downside\ Breakeven\ Point = Stock\ Price - Call\ Price$$

We can also display the outcomes of the previous scenarios in a table to make the potential outcomes clearer:

XYZ Price ($)	Stock Profit ($)	Call Price at Exp	Call Profit	Total Profit
40	−800	0	300	−500
45	−300	0	300	0
48	0	0	300	300
50	200	0	300	500
55	700	5	−200	500
60	1,200	10	−700	500

Table 2: Hypothetical Covered Call Payoffs for Company XYZ

Furthermore, we can use a graph to illustrate the payoff curve of such a trade.

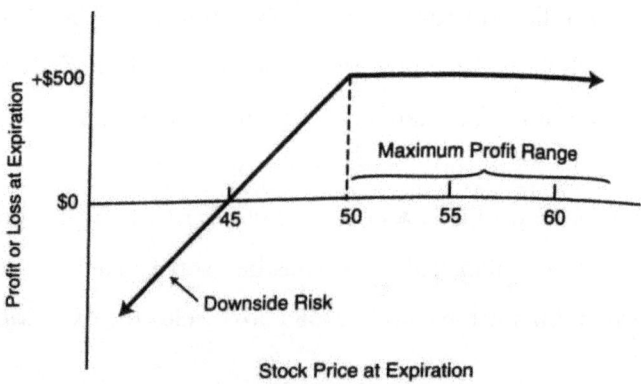

Figure 2: Covered Call Payoff Graph for Company XYZ

THE BUFFETT INDICATOR

Although I generally recommend against trying to time the market—meaning, the act of waiting to buy or sell investments for the sole purpose of trying to find the most favorable time to do so—there are times when it may be helpful to exercise more caution when investing.

These are often times when a bull market has prevailed for an extended period of time, and inevitably stocks have become overvalued. There are, of course, other ways to evaluate and gauge the risk of a coming recession, such as looking at unemployment rates, real GDP growth, earnings from various companies, and the previously mentioned yield curve. We will refrain from some of the more obvious measures and focus on just one for now. This indicator is called the Stock Market Capitalization to GPD Ratio, more colloquially known as the "Buffett Indicator," since its use was popularized by Warren Buffett. To calculate the total value of the US stock market, analysts often use the Wilshire 5000 Total Market Index. As its name suggests, this indicator is a comparison between the total value of the US stock market against the US GDP, expressed as a percentage. The formula is as follows:

$$Buffett\ Indicator = \frac{US\ Total\ Stock\ Market\ Capitalization}{US\ Total\ GDP} \times 100$$

As a general rule, a Buffett Indicator of around 50 percent suggests that the market is being "undervalued," while a Buffett Indicator over 100 percent suggests that the market is "overvalued." For example, before the Great Recession of 2008-9, the Buffett Indicator hit a high at just over 110 percent in September 2007 before plunging down to a low of about 59 percent in March 2009 after the recession hit. In what is perhaps a concerning situation, at the time of this writing in late 2019, the Buffett indicator stands at about 142 percent, potentially implying that the current stock market is highly overvalued. However, one should never fully rely on just one or a few indicators, since these are only meant to serve as guidelines in your making of investment decisions.

PORTFOLIO STRATEGIES

The then US Secretary of Defense Donald Rumsfeld said a famous phrase in 2002 in response to a question about the potential existence of weapons of mass destruction possessed by the Iraqi government. Expounding on the risks faced by the United States at the time, Rumsfeld stated,

> *There are known knowns; there are things we know we know. We also know there are known unknowns; that is to say we know there are some things we do not know. But there are also unknown unknowns—the ones we don't know we don't know. And if one looks throughout the history of our country and other free countries, it is the latter category that tend to be the difficult ones.*

These three categories of risk apply to the world of investing as well. In investing, there are known knowns, which are a company's published financial reports and fundamentals (assuming you live in a country where regulation is sufficient to ensure the accuracy of the numbers). There are known unknowns, such as the fact that technology will improve and cause industries to be disrupted or the inevitable occurrence of some type of market downturn in the future. And there are unknown unknowns, which include the exact timing of a market downturn's occurrence or the specific nature of how an industry might be disrupted. I generally recommend against "timing the market," meaning the act of attempting to find the correct time to buy or sell an investment to maximize returns. This is precisely because of the difficulty of accounting for unknown unknowns. It would be like if a person from the early 1900s had tried to predict what the world's most valuable company would be in 2019. One cannot possibly know with any degree of certainty the precise timing a recession will occur or how much the market will go down by if a recession occurs. These are unknown unknowns, and trying to time the market to buy in at the bottom is a hopeless endeavor. Generally, those who keep all their portfolio in cash waiting for a recession tend to miss out on massive stock market gains when their prediction for when a recession will occur inevitably proves to be wrong. However, this is not to say that you should do absolutely nothing to mitigate a potential recession. This is because the risk for a recession itself is a known unknown. That a recession will happen *at some point* is a known fact. Therefore, one can keep slightly more of one's portfolio in cash (usually at least 20 percent) and diversify positions to include more low-risk investments or hedges if one feels that a recession might occur soon. This is called a *defensive strategy*, and it may be a good idea to employ such a strategy when the economy flashes warning signs, such as a yield-curve inversion.

Here is a sample of some specific ways to set up an investment portfolio based on one's risk tolerance. Keep in mind that these are simply meant for reference purposes only and not meant to be followed exactly. They are, of course, subject to adjustment depending on your specific situation.

Investment type	Aggressive (%)	Moderate (%)	Conservative (%)	Defensive (%)
Bonds (Fixed Income)	0	10	20	20
Value/Dividend	10	20	25	20
High Growth	50	30	20	10
Speculative	25	15	5	0
Hedges	5	5	10	20
Cash	10	20	20	30

Table 3: Sample Breakdown of Investment Allocations by Risk Tolerance

To avoid the problem of missing the bottom of a crash or buying too early when trying to time the market, one can employ a strategy called "dollar-cost averaging." This is when an investor commits to buying into an investment in small, fixed chunks, no matter if the price increases or decreases. As the name suggests, over the long term, the cost basis on the investment would work out to be the average price of the investment over the same period of time. Although this strategy may not produce the highest potential returns, it essentially guarantees that it will never be the worst investment strategy, since it is by definition an average of the best- and worst-case scenarios.

THE RULE OF TWO

In the tech industry, there is a pattern that has emerged in recent times that I think would be of interest to the prospective long-term investor. I call this pattern the Rule of Two. The Rule of Two defines the two different and oppositional approaches to solving customers' problems that have both proven effective if implemented correctly. The two approaches are vertical integration and horizontal integration.

Vertical Integration

A strategy whereby a company owns or controls its suppliers, distributors, or retail locations in order to control its value or supply chain.

Horizontal Integration

Horizontal integration is the acquisition of a business operating at the same level of the value chain in a similar or different industry.

Horizontal integration is when a company becomes really dominant by opening its doors to many different intermediaries and works to integrate all those different groups or companies together to provide the customer with lots of choices but still a single place to access all those choices. An example that illustrates the difference is Apple versus Microsoft in the desktop operating system space; MacOS is designed to integrate and work with as many Apple products as possible for a controlled user experience, whereas Microsoft Windows's main selling point is its versatility and compatibility with most software out there. The same story is true between Apple and Google in smartphone operating systems. Where Google Android is highly customizable and available across a variety of smartphones, iOS is only available on iPhones, and its user experience seems highly controlled compared to Android's. Apple is often colloquially known as the "king of vertical integration," since it is by far the most successfully vertically integrated company in the world, though many other pairs of vertically and horizontally integrated industry leaders exist. Amazon can be considered a vertically integrated company that controls both the sale and fulfillment of products by having its own warehouses and delivering in Amazon-branded boxes. Often, customers do not even notice that their product on Amazon had originally come from a third-party retailer and that Amazon had only fulfilled the sale. Shopify seeks to become the horizontally integrated player in e-commerce by allowing business owners to set up their own websites and networks to sell their products, integrating systems from other companies to help customers achieve this. Notice how in all these comparisons these companies come in pairs. Thus, this is the Rule of Two. Formally, the Rule of Two states that there will often be two very successful companies in a new industry: one vertically integrated and the other horizontally integrated. Recognizing which two companies will emerge as the dominant forces in these two philosophies could be a great investment opportunity.

HOW TO INVEST YOUR FIRST $1,000

One of the questions that is most often on the mind of the beginner investor is, "How do I invest a small amount of money?" Unfortunately, normal people don't have hundreds of thousands of dollars in cash lying around, nor are they able to go to their parents and ask for a small loan of a million dollars. For me, I started investing when I was 18, when my dad gave me a loan of a thousand Canadian dollars, and I had to decide what I wanted to do with it. Looking back, my strategy back then wasn't the greatest. I picked a few stocks that had the nicest-looking analyst ratings section on CNN Money and dipped a few hundred in here and a few hundred there. This was before the age of commission-free trading, and each transaction cost me $10 to buy and another $10 to sell. I had put less than $200 into a few stocks, so it was safe to say that I didn't end up making any money. I wish I had known then what I know now, since there are ways that allow one to invest even a small amount of money (such as $1,000 or less) and still poise one's portfolio for growth in the future.

Pick One Company

Forget about how much money you have to invest with, for now. If you could only invest in one company, whether this meant throwing in a hundred or a million dollars, which company would it be? First of all, this would have to be a company that you really personally believe in, right? What people are passionate about varies drastically, but everyone inevitably has one or two things that they know and deeply understand. This could be technology, cars, makeup, whatever. There is at least one company out there that you believe brings a lot of value into your life. Now, of course, you should never forget to adopt the standard practices of properly evaluating a stock on a quantitative basis before buying it. Nonetheless, reflecting on the companies you have a deep positive opinion of will help you create a shortlist. Focus on companies that change lives or that have a sustained competitive advantage over their competitors. Once you've settled on a shortlist, pick your favorite from the list. Assuming that the company's other quantitative statistics fit within your criteria and level of risk tolerance, you should invest all of your $1,000 into it. Keep in mind that I am not advocating that everyone should do this. This is one of the riskiest strategies I suggest in this section; naturally, with the added risk it also offers one of the highest potential rewards.

Robo-advisor or Index Fund

If you're the type of person who is more on the risk-averse side, a robo-advising investment service could be a great choice. Robo-advisors are services that have passively managed portfolios catered to your risk tolerance. Typically, when you set up an investment account with a robo-advisor, it presents you with a questionnaire about your personal goals, retirement plans, and risk tolerance, then suggests a portfolio that fits your needs. In this sense, robo-advisors are very similar to traditional mutual funds, but the key difference is that robo-advisors typically have much lower fees: about 0.25 percent annually, on average. Again, since the portfolio is passive, this means you do no work; you may set it and forget it. If you want to go one step further and build a well-diversified portfolio with even lower fees, it may be a good idea for you to just buy into an index fund. There are many companies that run index funds, with one of the most famous being Vanguard, known for having some of the lowest management fees on their funds in the industry. For example, the Vanguard Total Stock Market Index Fund ($VTI) has a management expense ratio of only 0.03 percent.

Invest in Yourself

This is probably the investment route that will give you the highest amount of uncertainty but also offer the highest amount of potential reward. Every year, people pay tens of thousands of dollars to get postsecondary education, and they willingly do so because they believe that having a degree will allow them to make more money in the future compared to not having one. However, I think everyone has one or two hobbies that could potentially turn into fantastic businesses if they opt to spend time and money trying to build them, and these investments in pursuing passions could potentially require even less money upfront than going to school. Maybe you're an aspiring artist; maybe you race horses on the weekends; maybe you need a new camera to start your freelance photography side hustle. Now imagine if God were to drop out of the sky and give you some magical $100 bills that you could only spend if you were to use them for your potentially wealth-generating hobbies and interests. Imagine now that the $1,000 you have ready cannot be spent on anything that does not involve pursuing your passions. What would you do?

TAX-DEFERRED AND TAX-ADVANTAGED ACCOUNTS

There is definitely some truth to the statement that only two things are certain in life: death and taxes. Taxes are unavoidable if one wishes to avoid the inside of a jail cell. At the same time, taxes represent a huge obstacle on the path to financial independence. To help mitigate the negative effects of taxes on investors, here in North America, the governments of both the United States and Canada have offered some options for investors to have a slight edge over noninvestors via tax-deferred or tax-advantaged accounts. We will not go through the ideas behind some of these accounts and when it is better to use either one. If you reside outside of the United States or Canada, many other countries will often have similar tax-benefit account offerings, albeit under different names. Be sure to consult your own government's policies as to the specifics. Keep in mind that these are simply "vehicles" for your investments. This means that having a tax-deferred or tax-advantaged account is not an investment in and of itself, but rather is a special shelter for an individual to reduce their tax burden on their investments.

One still has to pick what kind of investments they would like to put inside these "vehicles."

Tax-Deferred Accounts

As the name suggests, these accounts allow the investor to save money into them before this money is taxed. This means that an individual may fund the account with money that can later be deducted from their total taxable income. For example, if you make $50,000 a year and you contribute $5,000 into a tax-deferred account, you can directly deduct that money from your income and only pay taxes on the remaining $45,000. The catch is that taxes must be paid when you withdraw the money out of the account at a later date, such as when you retire or after some other specified minimum age limit. Thus, the main advantage that tax-deferred accounts offer is that they reduce the amount of taxable income you are liable for during years when your income might be very high, such as in your 40s or 50s. As your income increases, the proportion of taxes you pay on the top portion of your income also increases. By deferring your taxes to when you retire, when your income is generally expected to drop compared to when you were working during your 40s or 50s, these accounts are a great way to artificially smooth out your income to take advantage of always being taxed at a lower rate. Another advantage of the tax-deferred account is access to more financial leverage. In a tax-deferred account, you may invest with money that would have otherwise gone toward paying taxes. Since the taxes on the deposit of the funds into the account have been deferred, those extra dollars essentially count as leverage that can be used for a much bigger gain later. Although those gains would still be taxed, combining this advantage with the aforementioned fact that income tends to go down during one's later years may still prove tax-deferred accounts more beneficial to the individual in the end when compared to other options.

In Canada, this type of tax-deferred account is known as a Registered Retirement Savings Plan (RRSP), while in the United States it is called an Individual Retirement Account (IRA).

Tax—Advantaged Accounts

These work the opposite way compared to a tax-deferred account. Rather than deferring their taxes to a later date, the individual pays taxes on the funds that are deposited into the account but pays no taxes on any of the money being withdrawn. This means that any money that one puts into such an account cannot be written off against the taxable income on one's tax return. Rather, it must come from money that has already been taxed. The main advantage to these types of accounts is that none of the gains on one's investments are taxed either. Therefore, these accounts are most suitable for young people, perhaps in their 20s or 30s, who have the power of time and compound interest on their side; they can benefit greatly from their exponentially high gains being tax free when they retire.

In Canada, this type of tax-advantaged account is known as a Tax-Free Savings Account (TSFA), while in the United States it is called a Roth Individual Retirement Account (Roth IRA).

THE OPPORTUNITY COSTS OF POSTSECONDARY EDUCATION

I started to learn how to play chess when I was in elementary school. In my own experience, what separates a bad chess player, a good chess player, and a great chess player is the ability to consider not only the immediate benefit of a move but also the space left behind by a piece after a player has made the move. For example, if a player is deciding whether to move his or her queen, a bad chess player will only look at the benefit of having the queen in her new spot. A good chess player might look at all the other pieces before deciding that the queen is the best piece to move. A great chess player will do all the aforementioned but also consider the drawbacks of no longer having the queen in her original spot after she has been moved. If one does not consider the space left behind by a moving piece, they may open themselves to a counterattack that had previously not been possible. This is the essence of opportunity cost: each time you choose to do something, you give up doing something else. In other words, *every action is not only comprised of the action itself but also the rejection of all its alternatives.* This idea is key to becoming successful not only in investing but in life in general. If you decide to see a movie, you are rejecting the idea of going to a concert or doing work during that time. Getting a postsecondary education is the exact same idea. By going to college or university, you are giving up the opportunity to simultaneously earn a full-time income. In other words, if you don't go to college, you could be working and making an income already. Therefore, the costs associated with postsecondary education include not only tuition and other mandatory fees but also the lost opportunity of a full-time income during those years. I am not saying that you shouldn't get postsecondary education. I went to university, myself, and it was by far the best learning experience that I have ever had in my life. However, a common problem that I've noticed among my fellow classmates is that many are unclear as to why they are in university or have unrealistic expectations about life. For example, I found that it was not uncommon for students to bash their own programs. They would complain about how they do not enjoy what they are learning and would rather do something else with their life, yet they remained in their program. They would spend tens of thousands of dollars or more on their four-year degrees while taking classes they don't like, then graduate only to try to find jobs in industries that they don't like. So, they not only give up a massive amount of money in tuition and the opportunity cost of a full-time salary during those years but also end up in jobs that make them miserable. Or, they may transfer to a different program in an attempt to find something that they like, all the while burning through more time and money. Another different problem is that some students often do not adequately plan for what to do once they graduate. For example, some people spend the aforementioned exorbitant tuition fees (most of them funded through student loans) on degrees that are not particularly in high demand, such as the liberal arts. Now, I do not mean to offend anyone who is studying or who has graduated with a liberal arts education. But you cannot deny that if your intention is to find a job in the liberal arts that makes enough income to quickly pay your debts off after you graduate, the odds are simply not in your favor. There are only so many museum curators and historians in the world, and both the demand for these jobs and their salaries are unlikely to eclipse that of full-stack developers any time soon. I understand your objections if studying the liberal arts is your passion—and I know that I have spent the majority of this book telling you that you should pursue your passions—but many professions in the arts do not require a university degree, and you should at least consider trying to pursue those passions without acquiring huge amounts of debt. Unless you have something very specific in mind that you want to achieve with a degree, you should consider if postsecondary education is right for you. In the end, numbers are numbers, and you need to make sure the numbers work realistically before you sign on the dotted line for a $100,000 loan.

ADDRESSING COMMON CRITICISMS OF FIRE

The idea of FIRE is not without its critics. In this section I share some of my opinions on the most frequently voiced criticisms against FIRE and defend my opinions in this book in much greater detail. A disclaimer here: I do admit that FIRE has many limitations and is not suitable for absolutely everyone. However, in my opinion, many criticisms of FIRE come from a fundamental lack of understanding about what exactly FIRE is and what it involves. I want to potentially clear up some of these misunderstandings now. If FIRE is a goal that you have in mind, my hope is that this section will erase at least a little of the doubt that you may have about whether you can actually achieve FIRE.

Criticism #1: I'm Giving Up Too Much; I Need My Daily Coffee

We probably all know or have at least heard of that one guy who decided to live off the grid, out of his minivan, giving up worldly luxuries such as a Netflix or Spotify subscription or frequent access to showers. And no, before you ask, that's not me. I don't live out of a van; I have both Netflix and Spotify Premium, and I have stable access to showers. Yet, when people think of frugal living, many picture the "no-spend hermit" in their mind's eye. Granted, some members of the FIRE community don't do ourselves any favors by badgering people to live like hermits and scolding them for the smallest splurge. Thus, many people who are unfamiliar with matters of personal finance mistakenly come to believe, "Oh, if I just give up my daily coffee habit and invested the money, that will allow me to retire early." If you believe that living frugally means giving up everything you love, that is completely backward and incorrect. The whole point is to get you to the point where you are comfortable spending $10 a day on coffee if you feel like it—but to get there, you need to first make some short-term sacrifices. If you truly believe that buying a coffee every morning is worth the extra convenience and money compared to making your own coffee, and that going to Starbucks is your life's passion and that you absolutely cannot give that up, then by all means keep your coffee habit. I want to focus on the root of the problem: overspending. Think about it this way: If you're willing to splurge, say, $7 on a single coffee, what else are you splurging on? As you can see, the $7 coffee is not the problem. I guarantee that you will never be $7 short of being able to retire when you want to or of being able to afford that Ferrari you've always wanted. You'll never look at the price of your dream house and go, "Damn, I wish I had $7 more, because then I'd be able to afford this." It's all about the mindset of overspending versus saving money; the daily coffee is just a symptom. By focusing unduly on whether to give the coffee up, one misses the point of the whole FIRE mindset. The same goes for any other expensive hobbies you may have. In university, I started a FIRE club and made a mailer on my university's Reddit page advertising the club. On one of the comments I received, an anonymous student noted that he did not want to join the club because he had been criticized by the FIRE community for spending lots of money on his car-modding hobby in the past. I felt bad for him. The way I see it, you can spend the next 40 or so years working a nine-to-five job and mod cars on the weekends and after work, or you can try to become financially independent in 10–15 years and devote the rest of your life to doing whatever you want, including modding cars if that's what you want. The whole point of

FIRE is to enable you to free up more time and spend more money on the things that you love.

Criticism #2: Even If I Save Money and Retire Early, I'd Still Not Have Enough Money

The argument goes something like this: "If I save money like crazy and get to have $1 million invested in dividend stocks that pay around 3-4 percent annually in dividends by the time I'm 35, that's still only $30,000-40,000 per year, which is not enough for me to live off, especially if I have a family."

While this argument seems convincing at first, we have to keep in mind some of the assumptions being made here:

1. You only invest in dividend-paying stocks
2. Your dividend-stock-only portfolio has zero capital gains
3. You plan on fully living off your dividends
4. Besides your dividends, once you retire, your income will be zero for the rest of your life

If all these assumptions are true, then I agree that it will be very difficult to become financially independent even if you managed to have $1 million invested. However, to ease your worries, these assumptions are very unrealistic, in my opinion.

I've already illustrated some of the differences between growth and value investing, and dividend investing usually falls more on the side of value investing. I believe that it is a mistake to be a dividend-only investor, since some of the biggest gains in the stock market historically have come from growth stocks. Therefore, it is generally a bad idea to have *all* of your portfolio be dividend stocks, since you will most likely miss out on very high gains from growth companies.

Second, we are assuming that your portfolio experiences zero capital gains. This is very unrealistic even if you are a dividend-only investor since, as we mentioned earlier, the stock market as a whole tends to yield about 8-10 percent annually in the long term. Even with a conservative estimate of 7 percent annual capital gains, over the long term your returns would still be quite significant. It is generally accepted that if one is invested in a broad-market index fund, one can withdraw 4 percent of one's portfolio's value per year and do this indefinitely without ever decreasing the principal on their portfolio. This is known as the 4 percent rule, and it goes to show that the assumption of zero capital gains is unrealistic. Another quick estimate you can do right now is called the Rule of 72. If you take the number 72 and divide it by a given annual rate of return and round it to the nearest integer, you will get back the approximate number of years it would take for your money to double. Expanding upon our previous estimate of an annual return of 7 percent, 72 divided by 7 is about 10.28; in just over 10 years, your money will double, assuming that you compounded your returns and did not withdraw any money along the way. If we turn the rate of return up to 15 percent annually, the Rule of 72 tells us it will only take 4.8 years for your money to double. It's clear that even getting close to a 15 percent annual return will put you well on the track to financial independence.

Last, you should always look to diversify your income sources. It would be a bad idea to fully rely on your dividends to sustain yourself. Also, we are assuming that once you have a $1 million portfolio, you would opt to lay on the couch and watch TV forever for the rest of your life without making a single dime. I think for the most part, even if one were to have a $1 million investment portfolio, one generally does not opt to do *absolutely nothing productive* for the rest of their lives. I think people who believe that retiring at 35 means that you'll be a lazy bum forever are mistaken in that belief. Once you have, let's say, $35,000 a year coming in as dividend money, you can take on that job as a part-time car detailer or painter and be okay with making $40,000 a year because you have an alternative source of income. I know you're now going to say, "But that's not really retirement." While that's technically true, I would in fact count it as retirement in my book, especially compared to the constraints facing a typical nine-to-five office worker around the same age range.

Criticism #3: There's No Way I Can Save That Much Money to Retire in 15 Years

Assuming you want to retire in 15 years and you start off with nothing, and assuming a market rate of return of about 8 percent annually, you'd have to invest about $2,900 per month, every month, for all those 15 years to get to over $1 million. I understand how this would be a tall order for most people, and people argue that FIRE is unrealistic as a result. However, throughout this book I have illustrated techniques to help you beat the market. Remember, the $2,900 per month number is under the assumption that you make the same return as the market average. This means that you literally do no research and invest completely passively by throwing all your money into an index fund and never looking at it again until your 15 years are up. By being a bit smarter with your money and picking individual stocks using some of the techniques in this book, combined with lots of your own research and time, it is not unreasonable to achieve a 12 percent annual return. If we assume 12 percent and keep the retirement goal of $1 million in 15 years, the monthly contribution drops down to just over $2,000 per month, which is much more within the grasp of most people. As previously mentioned, we had set a goal of getting a 15 percent annual return. In that case, to get to $1 million in 15 years would only take about $1,500 per month. One last assumption that I should bring to your attention is that we assumed you start off with absolutely nothing. In the span of time that I was in university, I managed to accumulate over $10,000 USD for an investment portfolio from the money I earned doing internships. If we assume that you start off with $10,000 and use a 15 percent annual return, again with the goal of getting to $1 million in 15 years, your monthly contribution is now only about $1,360. I encourage you to crunch some numbers yourself; there are numerous free compound interest calculators you can play around with online, and these will help encourage you to beat the stock market.

Part Four: Lessons, Stories and Analects

The following is a small collection of stories that may not have any direct relationship to the topic of FIRE but that will help you better understand the nature of how money works and hopefully provide some valuable insights into the world of finance.

TIMES WHEN COMPANIES DIDN'T DO THEIR MATH

In my final year of high school, I took an introductory calculus course. I was rather surprised to recognize one of my friends in that class, since I had recently found out that he had accepted an offer from a nearby university to study music, so taking a calculus course was completely unnecessary for him. I asked him why he had decided to take this course. There were much easier ways to get one more credit for graduation, if that's what he needed. He replied that he wanted to "see how hard math can get" before he died. If I remember correctly, he did not end up with a very high mark in the calculus course in the end. However, I appreciated and admired his drive for a challenge. He had a genuine interest in math and wasn't afraid to make mistakes. In contrast, I found that most other people in that course did not take it out of interest but simply because the program they wanted to get into at university required them to take the course; they would forget everything they learned as soon as the exam was over. Perhaps I am biased, as I ended up going to university for math—though I'm not saying you need to be an expert in calculus to succeed in life—but having just a basic understanding of math can go a long way in situations where you least expect math to be helpful. Here are some real-life stories of what can go wrong when even executives at big companies forget what they had learned in high school.

Your Own Fleet of Private Jets

In 1981, American Airlines, one of the biggest airline companies in the United States, needed to raise some quick cash to combat increasing costs associated with its operations. The answer was to offer the Unlimited American Airlines AAirpass. As its name suggests, the pass offered unlimited first-class flights on any American Airlines flight for the price of $250,000 for a single pass and $150,000 for an optional add-on companion pass. The total cost, then, for two passes would be $400,000, or about $1.2 million dollars in 2019 when adjusted for inflation. The intention was to aim this pass at business executives who would use it for their frequent business trips. Initially thought to be a failure with only 66 customers, the low popularity of the AAirpass turned out to be somewhat of a silver lining for American Airlines customers; the airline would spend the next few decades desperately trying to take back the unlimited AAirpasses. The problem was that this deal was simply too good for customers. American Airlines had grossly underestimated the extent to which the passes would be used, and the price of the pass was simply too low for the added costs the customers brought to the airline. Furthermore, the terms of the original contract for the AAirpass were rather loose, and the pass gave out generous benefits on top of unlimited first-class travel. Those benefits included access to the American Airlines Admiral's Club series of airport lounges, where members could get unlimited free food and drink. Essentially, this pass gave the holder a degree of freedom akin to owning an entire fleet of private jets. One of the most famous owners of the AAirpass was an investment banker named Steve Rothstein who used his pass to book over 10,000 first-class flights. Often, Rothstein would use his pass to fly from Chicago to London, England, for lunch, and fly back the same day. Sometimes, he would book a flight from Chicago to Providence, Rhode

Island, just to get his favorite sandwich from a particular store that he was well-acquainted with. Each flight would cost American Airlines hundreds or even thousands of dollars in fuel and tax costs on top of lost sales. And Rothstein wasn't the only person doing this. Many other pass holders flew much more than expected. Further exacerbating the issue, fuel costs back in the 1980s were about 50 percent higher than in 2019 even after adjusting for inflation. It was estimated that each pass was costing American Airlines $1 million per year. Over the course of the next few decades, American Airlines would be entangled in various court battles to try to revoke the pass from its holders. The results of these legal battles were mixed, and several prominent public figures, such as Michael Dell (founder of Dell Computers) and Mark Cuban (owner of the Dallas Mavericks) are known to still hold the pass.

That Time when Pepsi Promised a $33 Million Harrier Jet

A young man in sunglasses puts his leather jacket on. Underneath his unzipped jacket, he's wearing a t-shirt with the Pepsi logo on it. Each item's value in Pepsi points is displayed on screen. T-shirt, 75 points; leather jacket, 1,450 points; sunglasses, 175 points. The camera changes to a typical-looking American middle school, where three boys eagerly browse the Pepsi prizes catalogue to see the myriad rewards being offered in exchange for Pepsi points. They hear a loud hum, and a black shadow graces across the sky. The scene changes again, this time to what appears to be a boring lecture in a classroom. The windows are open, and a gust of wind sends papers flying everywhere. The loud hum outside only becomes louder. People run and duck for cover, just in time to see the young man land his Harrier jet vertically in a patch of grass in the schoolyard. The bottom of the frame displays the price of the jet: 7,000,000 Pepsi points.

The "Drink Pepsi, Get Stuff" ad campaign of 1995 was initially considered a huge success. The idea was to give out "Pepsi Points" that purchasers of Pepsi products could then exchange for cool stuff. However, during the ad campaign, Pepsi inadvertently made a mistake when they displayed the price of a Harrier jet in Pepsi points. Pepsi had a program where one could buy Pepsi points for 10 cents each. So, effectively, according to the price that Pepsi had set themselves, a Harrier jet would effectively cost $700,000. According to average estimates at the time, a Harrier jet cost approximately $33 million if bought at market price. This was noticed by a man named John Leonard, who was at the time a 21-year-old business student. Within a year, Leonard had gathered enough investors to cough up the approximately $700,000 needed, and he mailed a check to Pepsi with the intention to order a Harrier jet. Leonard promptly received an apology letter from Pepsi, stating that the promise of a Harrier jet was mainly a joke and that it was not actually in the list of prizes being offered. Clearly, Pepsi had not intended for anyone to actually single-handedly spend enough money to get to 7,000,000 points. Leonard, however, was completely serious: he proceeded to sue Pepsi for breach of contract—the commercial had indeed seemingly stated that a Harrier jet was being offered for 7,000,000 points. The case would drag on in the courts for three years until the courts finally ruled in Pepsi's favor, stating that "no objective person could reasonably have concluded that the commercial actually offered consumers a Harrier Jet." Although in the end Pepsi managed to avoid having to give out a Harrier Jet, soon after Leonard sued the company, Pepsi updated its commercials such that a Harrier jet would now cost 700,000,000 Pepsi points, in what can be considered an admission of a mistake—and perhaps a show of fear.

The US Government's Terrible Mistake Selling $1 for $1

In 2005, the US government wanted a way to boost the use of its $1 coin. Although coins cost more to make than bills, a coin lasts much longer than a bill, and the $1 coin would save the government an estimated $13 billion in production costs over the course of 30 years if a full changeover from bills to coins were implemented. Thus, a brilliant idea was hatched, and the US government instructed the treasury to begin production of a new wave of dollar coins. In 2008, the US mint began an incentive to encourage people to start using the dollar coins. The mint would offer to sell the coins at face value and ship them for free anywhere in the United States. On the surface, nothing seemed wrong with this offer. Sure, the government would lose a bit of money having to ship heavy coins, but the loss was acceptable if that's what it took to put all the coins in circulation. However, as the old saying goes, the devil is in the details. The US mint made one crucial mistake in this offering that would come back to haunt them for years to come: they accepted credit cards. In the United States, a typical credit card offers about one cent per dollar spent as travel points or cashback. People realized that they could buy the coins, have them shipped for free, then immediately deposit the coins into the bank and pay their credit cards back. This process can be done an arbitrary number of times and is really only limited by one's credit card's limit. A man named Brad Wilson reportedly racked up over four million frequent flyer miles over an eight-month period by buying over $3 million worth of coins. The US mint finally began to catch on to what people were doing when their stockpiles of dollar coins only increased with time, as people kept depositing them back. To combat this, the mint sometimes sent angry letters to people making large purchases of coins, demanding to know why they wanted to buy so many. These letters were largely ignored by the recipients, since what they were doing was not illegal. Eventually, the mint started to process the purchases through credit cards as cash advances, which do not earn any reward points. The dollar-coin program would drag on for years before ending in failure in 2011, when it was finally canceled. By that time, the Federal Reserve had accumulated over a billion dollars' worth of coins, all of which had never been used.

***

We have already touched on the concept of expected value earlier on in the book, and the aforementioned few stories are perfect examples of what can go wrong when companies make mistakes in valuating their offers against how much benefit they will receive in return for their offers. The main takeaway here is that these are multibillion-dollar organizations who have made simple mathematical errors that proved to be either disastrous or near disastrous. Each decision, whether it was offering an unlimited airpass or a Harrier jet, or even selling dollar coins at face value, most likely went through many high-ranking executives at their respective organizations before it was approved. And none of them caught these mistakes. In your own life, you must be vigilant in preventing yourself from making similar simple mathematical errors. Keep in mind that you do not need to be a mathematician for this. If anyone just sits down and thinks about any of these situations for just a second, they will soon realize their potential for gain if they manage to take advantage of the situations. Second, in life, you will inevitably encounter at least one of these opportunities, in which benefit can be gained with very little or no risk. In finance this is known as *arbitrage*, and taking advantage of these opportunities will accelerate you on the path to FIRE. It is your job to constantly look for arbitrage opportunities in your everyday life.

FINANCIAL BUBBLES AND CRISES

When the topic of financial bubbles comes up, most people think of the great stock market crash of 1929, which sparked the Great Depression, a period that lasted all the way until the end of World War II. However, several financial bubbles have occurred both before and after 1929, each with its own unique set of circumstances and end results. We will now go through some of the most significant ones. Keep in mind that financial bubbles are simply a consequence of human nature and that they will occur again in the future.

The Dutch Tulip Crisis

In 1631 the Dutch Empire was at its zenith during a period known as the Dutch Golden Age, in which the Netherlands became the most dominant power in the world in terms of art, science, and, especially, trade. Amsterdam became home to many of the world's wealthiest merchants, who displayed their wealth in elaborate flower gardens surrounding their mansions. One flower, however, was the most prized of all: the tulip. First introduced to Europe from the Ottoman Empire in the 1550s, tulips were unlike any other flower that existed in Europe at the time. In a rather odd coincidence, some tulips became infected with a virus from the genus *Potyvirus*, now commonly referred to as the "tulip-breaking virus," which causes the colors of tulip petals to split to form multicolored petals. Often, these tulips have red or orange flamelike streaks that rise up from the base of the flower and meander throughout the petal. These multicolored tulips became the most sought-after tulips due to their exotic look. By the mid-1630s, the price of the tulip had risen so much that it became to attract the attention of traders and speculators. Often, these "investors" had no interest in owning the tulips themselves; they simply sought to gain financial wealth by buying into tulip future contracts and selling them to the next highest bidder for a profit. Due to the nature of future contracts, during all this time very few tulips actually changed hands. People simply traded the contracts, and the price of tulips kept rising. This pattern would continue for years, as there was always someone willing to pay a higher price for tulips. The price of the tulip hit its peak in early 1637, when the price of one bulb was being sold for more than 10 times the annual salary of an average Dutch skilled worker. Then it all came crashing down. In February of 1637, a bulb went unsold for the first time ever; the Tulip Mania was over. The price of tulips promptly collapsed, and many people lost their entire fortunes overnight.

The Great Recession of 2008—9

In 2008, on what seemed like a normal September weekend, Warren Buffett received a call from a banker at Lehman Brothers. It had become vividly clear for a while now to the executives at the American financial giant Lehman Brothers that they were in deep trouble. A few months earlier, in March of 2008, the CEO of Lehman Brothers, Richard Fuld Jr., had called Buffett to try to enlist his help in saving the company from bankruptcy. Buffett went down to the Lehman Brothers office later that day and pored through the company's Form 10-K, an annual report that details all a company's financial positions. Upon reading hundreds of pages of reports and encountering numerous red flags about the company's financial position, Buffett determined that there was nothing he could do to save Lehman Brothers. Lehman Brothers would file for bankruptcy on the weekend of September 13, 2008. The Friday preceding the same weekend that marked Lehman Brothers' bankruptcy, another American financial giant, American International Group (AIG), had also reached out to Buffett for help. In a similar sequence of events as Lehman Brothers, it was clear to Buffett that there was simply no way to prevent AIG from running out of cash within days. The company had made very foolish financial decisions, and its demise was now inevitable.

In retrospect, the root causes of the financial crisis of 2008-9 had been in the making for the better part of the preceding decade. Modern economists and professional analysts have concluded that one of the main causes of the crisis (and the recession that followed) is what is known as the Agency Problem, which occurred heavily in the mortgage market that led up to 2008. Usually, borrowers who apply for mortgages must go through a credit score evaluation and other checks that banks perform on borrowers to determine the latter's ability to pay back their mortgages. Obviously, the riskier the borrower is deemed to be, the less money the bank will be willing to loan to them. However, in the years leading up to 2008, the banks noticed something that gave them an opportunity to drastically increase their revenues. They packaged the mortgages into a bundle called a Collateralized Debt Obligation (CDO) and sold it off to investors. These investors included pension funds, insurance companies, and other financial institutions. In theory, this seemed like a great idea at first. Banks would get their money right away, and investors would take the risk in case the borrowers defaulted on their mortgages, as the investors now own the debt. Many investors who bought into these CDOs did not truly understand what they were buying.

Many had the false belief that these were safe investments, since mortgages were generally regarded as a safe bet. People tended to pay their mortgages first and above all else, after all. However, if one had looked closer, one would have found that many of the CDOs comprised what are known as "subprime" mortgages, meaning that the borrower had less-than-ideal credit and was likely not in a position to be able to make monthly mortgage payments in full. The agency problem arises from the misalignment of incentives between the banks, investors, and borrowers. Borrowers would naturally be more inclined to take out as big of a mortgage as the banks would give them, even if they had bad credit. This problem was further exacerbated by the fact that many banks offered so-called "teaser rates," where the mortgage interest rate would be very low in the beginning of the loan, which caused the initial monthly payments to be miniscule. Borrowers would get used to paying very little each month on their mortgage, until the teaser rate inevitably expired and the rate returned to normal, causing a sudden spike in their monthly mortgage obligations. Many borrowers would be unprepared for this sudden, drastic change, and they would default on their mortgages. The banks became more and more willing to give out large mortgages to people who really couldn't afford them, since they could turn around and sell these mortgages off to investors for a profit anyway. Therefore, the banks were incentivized to approve as many mortgages as they could, even if the applications came from subprime borrowers. In an effort to protect themselves against the mortgage holders defaulting, many investors would purchase Credit Default Swaps (CDS), which are essentially insurance contracts that protect the debt holder in case the borrower defaults, which effectively shifted the risk of default onto issuers of CDS's rather than the CDO investors themselves. One of the companies that issued the largest number of CDS's was, of course, AIG.

At first, AIG had been raking in billions of dollars issuing CDS's. It was easy money, and no one at AIG ever thought that people would stop paying their mortgages—until they did. The housing market began to sink in 2007, and AIG was seeing its cash reserves quickly deplete. On September 15, 2008, the same day that Lehman Brothers announced its bankruptcy, AIG finally ran out of money completely. The collapse of Lehman Brothers and AIG triggered the worst financial crisis in a decade, and its impact can still be felt today.

The South Sea Bubble

In 1710, after much political maneuvering, Robert Harley was appointed to the role of Chancellor of the Exchequer for the British government. His exuberance, however, was quickly dashed when it became apparent that Britain was in deep debt. Not only had years of war and improper bookkeeping left huge debt loads, no one was even quite sure exactly how much money the government owed. Harley faced the monumental task of keeping the government afloat in a sea of debt. The government was in a deadlock, as the liberal Whigs and the conservative Tories were blocking each other's legislation at every opportunity, so raising taxes was out of the question. The years of war had soured Britain's relationship with other European powers, so it would be difficult to find external funding. At the time, the Bank of England was controlled by the liberal Whigs, and they refused to help Harley, who was a conservative. All this left Harley with very few options; he'd have to get a little more creative. The man to answer the call was a man named John Blunt, the owner of the Hollow Sword Blades Company. Blunt had made a fortune using some unscrupulous tactics that would surely be illegal today, and probably were even back then. The British government had confiscated large amounts of Irish

Catholics' land, and Blunt wanted to buy some. However, he quickly realized he did not have the cash for it. In an effort to raise quick money, he offered to trade shares of his company for British army debentures: bonds that the military would issue if they ran out of money to pay for something. These army debentures were worth very little, since there was no feasible way for a private citizen or company to collect on the debt; the military does not exactly allow one to waltz in and repossess its assets. As a result, army debentures were effectively not backed by anything and traded much below their face value. Before making the offer, Blunt had secretly bought up a large amount of army debentures, and when word was out that he was willing to trade shares for them, the offer was too good to refuse. The price of the army debentures skyrocketed as demand increased, and more and more people elected to take Blunt up on his offer. Furthermore, as the price of the debentures rose, Blunt used the newly inflated price of his debentures to trade directly for the land that he wanted to buy, since it was being offered by the government. With this newfound wealth, Blunt loaned part of his new money to the government, and with this a partnership formed between Harley and Blunt.

The "South Sea" at the time of the South Sea Company referred to South America and its nearby islands, since most of the South Pacific Ocean was unknown to Britain at the time. The South Sea Company was a scheme formed by Harley and Blunt both to try to solve the national debt crisis and undermine the power of the Bank of England. The promise of this company was to replicate the success of the East India Company, but in South America. The idea was that the government would exchange its debt for shares in the South Sea Company. The company would charge the government a lower interest rate than what they were currently paying, and the interest collected would be used as a dividend to pay shareholders with. However, in order to convince the government debt-holders to give up their debt in exchange for shares in an unknown company, they must be convinced that the shares would ultimately be worth more than the debt they held. Thus, Harley and Blunt began an aggressive marketing campaign to promote the potential riches the South Sea Company would bring. In retrospect, this idea had a huge problem to begin with. All the ports in Central and South America were controlled by Spain, with whom Britain was then at war. Harley and Blunt's solution to this was to sue for peace with Spain. Through some political maneuvering, they finally managed to get the government to make peace with Spain. However, the terms and accommodations that Spain gave were less than ideal. The South Sea Company was only given the—questionably lucrative—right to trade slaves in the South Sea and the right to send one ship a year to each of Spain's ports. Clearly, this would not be even close to matching what the South Sea Company had promised.

In 1714, Queen Anne passed away, she was succeeded by King George I and a new government. Harley fell out of favor with the new monarch and was promptly booted out of office. With sole control of the company, Blunt could now implement the next phase of pumping the value of the South Sea Company up even further. Through new legislation, the government allowed the South Sea Company to issue an amount of shares equal in value to its debt load. But, as the share price rose, the amount of shares needed to cover the debt would decrease, and Blunt could now sell off the extra shares for a profit. Thus, assuming the price of the shares kept rising, more money was to be made the larger the amount of debt that the government was willing to trade for South Sea shares. Eventually, through a series of bribes to members of parliament, Blunt managed to convince the government to consolidate its remaining £31 million worth of debt and exchange it for shares in the South Sea Company. As prominent public figures started to buy into the stock, it only further inflated demand for it and its stock price. The company was soon valued at £300 million, which was multiple times higher than the entire British national economy at the time. Adjusted for inflation, at its peak the South Sea Company was valued somewhere in the range of four trillion in 2019 US dollars. This was, of course, unsustainable, and the share price began to collapse in 1720 as the bubble finally burst. By this time, the company still had not made a single cent trading in the South Sea. Sir Isaac Newton, the famous physicist, was famously known to have been an investor in the South Sea Company; he supposedly lost an amount somewhere in the range of £20,000-30,000 in the collapse of its stock price, an amount worth approximately $3 million USD in today's dollars. He was famously quoted saying, "I can calculate the movement of the stars, but not the madness of men."

WATERSHED MOMENTS OF MISSED OPPORTUNITIES

The term "watershed moment" is used to describe an event in history that marks a turning point— a different decision made by one person or a small group of people at that point would have resulted in a vastly different outcome, changing the course of history. The term comes from the geological feature of a "watershed": the piece of land that divides two rivers or any two distinct bodies of water that are about to join. We will now look at some watershed moments in the business world and imagine what the world might have looked like if slightly different decisions had been made.

Blockbuster Passes Up Buying Netflix

If you're old like I am, you may remember that in a distant past there once existed a company called Blockbuster; you may have even visited one of its stores. The success of Blockbuster's business model relied on a series of actions that needed to be performed by the consumer that would be unimaginable to most of us today. Blockbuster was a videos and movies store; you would go to a physical store location, pick out a movie that you liked in the format of VHS, DVD, or Blu-ray, then line up to pay a small fee to rent the movie for a night or two. A common problem was that people would often forget to return the movie on time and be charged a small late fee. However, most of the time, this was still more cost-efficient than buying a DVD outright, and most people would only watch a movie once, anyway. It was a good idea, but as the company executives soon realized, the world was beginning to change, and Blockbuster had fallen asleep at the wheel.

In 1996, Reed Hastings had just completed the sale of his software company to a larger firm for a cool $700 million USD. Now a man of great wealth, he began to look for the next big opportunity. The next big thing would become clear to him in 1997, when he rented a copy of the movie *Apollo 13* on VHS from Blockbuster and forgot to return it. He was slapped with a $40 late fee. There had to be a better way for consumers to enjoy movies, he thought. He enlisted the help of his friend Marc Randolph, and together they founded a company named "Netflix." Originally, Netflix did not have the internet streaming services it would later become famous for. The technology in 1997 simply did not allow for streaming to be feasible. Instead, Hastings focused on the emerging DVD market, which provided more capacity and was less bulky than the VHS tapes that were popular at the time. Netflix would become a DVD mailing service; customers would pay a fee online and have a DVD mailed to their home. Since DVDs are small and light, they can be packaged in envelopes and mailed for the same cost as a first-class mail stamp. Utilizing his skills and experience in software, Hastings and the rest of his team developed an algorithm that recommended movies to customers depending on what they had previously watched. This feature was practically unheard of back in 1997 and would become a hallmark for Netflix in the future. The business was very successful; it would later introduce a plan that allowed customers to pay a monthly fee to have four DVDs simultaneously and the ability to hold on to them for as long as they paid the monthly fee. In September 2000, Netflix was bleeding cash and needed to look for ways to raise some capital. Netflix approached Blockbuster for a strategic partnership, and Blockbuster arranged a meeting in Dallas, a long-haul flight away from California, and the management only gave Hastings and the other executives at Netflix less than 12 hours' notice. Barry McCarthy, then the CFO of Netflix, balked at this inconsiderate meeting suggestion: a last-minute flight to Dallas like this would cost at least $20,000, and the company was on track to record more than a $50 million loss that year. Hastings decided that it was worth the chance, so they decided to go in the end. The deal that Netflix offered Blockbuster would effectively integrate Netflix's DVD mailing service into Blockbuster's traditional movie-rental service as well as drop the name Netflix altogether in favor of "Blockbuster.com." The price Netflix offered Blockbuster for this deal was fifty million dollars. The CEO of Blockbuster at the time, John Antioco, was struggling to hold his laughter in. Clearly, Antioco did not seriously consider the offer; he did not even bother to make a counteroffer. Antioco believed at the time that Netflix was only poised to serve a small "niche market"; furthermore, Netflix had yet to turn a profit. The founders of Netflix left the meeting and spent the ride back to the airport in silence. Over the better part of the next decade, Netflix would continue to expand its business. After having shunned Netflix, Blockbuster decided to partner with Enron Broadband, a division of Enron, in an ironic twist of fate. Those familiar with history will know of the Enron Scandal in 2001, which exposed Enron's involvement in massive acts of financial fraud committed over the course of many years, which ultimately led to the demise of the company. Blockbuster, for its part, could not have known about the fraud, but it was nevertheless doubly unlucky to have both passed up buying Netflix and partnered with a fraudulent company. In the mid-2000s, the DVD wars were really beginning to heat up: Wal-Mart joined the fray, as well as smaller companies such as Redbox, which offered DVD rentals completely through vending machines and was able to undercut the competition because of its low costs. In 2008, the new CEO of Blockbuster Jim Keyes said a quote that has now become infamous. Keyes famously stated, "Neither Redbox nor Netflix are even on the radar screen in terms of competition, it's more Wal-Mart and Apple." But by that time, the situation had already begun to turn sour for Blockbuster. Sales had begun to decline, and the company was forced to shut down more stores as well as rid themselves of the late fees that represented a large chunk of their revenue. These efforts were too little too late. Blockbuster filed for bankruptcy in September of 2010, almost exactly 10 years after that fateful meeting in Dallas.

That Time Yahoo! Almost Bought Google

In the mid-1990s, the world was mesmerized by a revolutionary new technology called the Internet. One of the earliest and biggest players on the Internet was Yahoo!, which ran an internet directory that had curated lists of the most popular websites on the Internet. Yahoo! became famous for popularizing banner ads, often described as "billboards on the Internet." The ads brought in a tremendous amount of revenue, and competitors were forced to follow suit. In 1996, two PhD candidates from Stanford University named Larry Page and Sergey Brin developed an algorithm named PageRank, which proved very effective at searching the web based on keywords that a user would type in. Page and Brin approached Yahoo! the following year with an offer to buy PageRank off them for just $1 million. The Yahoo! executives balked at this idea, though. At the time, they were focused on ways to display more banner ads and giving the user a quick way to find the website they were looking for, which would cause users to spend less time on Yahoo!, thus decreasing the amount of banner ads that can be shown, would in turn cause a decline in Yahoo!'s revenue. Not giving up on their idea and what they had built even after being refused by Yahoo!, Page and Brin decided to start their own website focused on Internet search. They named the company "Google," and it quickly gained a loyal fanbase due to its commitment of providing high quality and accurate search results. Yahoo! was still rather unfazed by Google's success, since it still had massive revenue coming in from banner ads. Google, on the other hand, had seemingly made the inexplicable decision to pass up the opportunity to make massive amounts of advertising revenue by choosing to not display ads on its homepage. Google's homepage seemed painfully simple to Yahoo!; it was just the Google logo and a search bar, and that was about it. It is worth noting that Google did not shun advertising altogether, since it still needed to make money to sustain itself. However, Google's approach to advertising was to allow advertisers to list their web links at the top of search results and integrate them to seem as if they were part of the results. This approach was less intrusive than banner ads, and Google continued to grow at an ever-increasing pace. In 2001, Yahoo! had survived the aftermath of the Dot-com Bubble but had suffered greatly. The board of directors at Yahoo! decided that it was time to make a shift in the direction that the company was going, and they brought Terry Semel over as the new CEO. Semel had been the former CEO of Warner Bros.; despite having little experience in the tech industry, he tried to shake up the company in a fundamental way. Semel could see that the popularity of the banner ad was declining and concluded that Yahoo! also needed a strong presence in the search game. The following year, Semel offered to buy Google for $3 billion. But this time, Page and Brin knew that they had the upper hand in the negotiations. They returned with a counteroffer of $5 billion. Yahoo! was still recovering from the Dot-com crash in 2002, and the price seemed unacceptable. Semel refused the offer and decided that he would purchase smaller companies to help him get into search. Yahoo! purchased Inktomi, the second-best search engine at the time besides Google, as well as Overture, which specialized in paid search. The integration of Inktomi and Overture with Yahoo! proved a lot more troublesome than previously expected, and another two years would pass before the integration was complete. By that time, Google's revenues had exceeded twice that of Yahoo!'s. Yahoo!'s decline seemed inevitable. In 2017, the majority of Yahoo! was acquired by Verizon Communications for $4.48 billion. By comparison, at the time of this writing in late 2019, the market cap of Alphabet Inc., Google's parent company, has reached over $850 billion USD.

How Volvo Could've Owned 10 percent of Norway's Oil

The economy of Norway had mostly comprised and been sustained by shipping and fishing for centuries. In the aftermath of World War II, Norway's infrastructure had suffered greatly, and the country was struggling on its path to recovery. In 1959, the Royal Dutch Shell Company was looking for oil in the Netherlands. Although they did not discover any oil, they inadvertently stumbled upon what would later be named the Groningen gas field—the largest deposit of natural gas in Europe. The discovery of the Groningen gas field sparked renewed interest in the potential of finding oil in the North Sea, since the geology of the two areas is similar. For decades, the prospect of oil in the North Sea had been largely ignored due to the North Sea's infamously stormy weather, which added to the cost of surveying the area. The oil rigs that would have to be built in the North Sea needed to withstand waves of up to 15 meters and winds of up to 110 kilometers per hour. The high barrier to entry prevented interest in oil exploration from developing, especially given Norway's still-recovering economy. However, everything was about to change. In 1969, Norway hit its first jackpot with the discovery of the Ekofisk oil field. A year later, the UK quickly followed with the discovery of an even larger oil field, the Forties oil field. Many more discoveries of oil in the North Sea would follow in the coming decades. The Norwegian government took an aggressive stance on the oil companies drilling in the North Sea, maintaining a minimum of 50 percent state ownership of any Norwegian oil company and taxing the companies at 78 percent. With this newfound wealth, the government created the Norwegian Sovereign Wealth Fund, which would become the largest sovereign wealth fund in the world.

In the 1920s, Sweden was on the rise. Having stayed neutral in World War I, the Swedish company SKF had sold ball bearings to both the Allies and Central Powers and made a fortune. After the war, SKF used the extra money they made to fund various side projects, the most notable being their first attempt at entering the automotive market with a new brand, Volvo. When World War II broke out, Sweden remained neutral once again and played the same game that had worked out so well for them during World War I. After the war ended, and while the rest of Europe struggled to pick up the pieces, Sweden was uniquely positioned to take advantage of the world's postwar recovery phase, since its factories had never been bombed. But by the 1950s, after Volvo had established itself as a household name in Europe and even in the United States, it was clear that competition was heating up, and Volvo was too small to be able to effectively compete. After several failed attempts at a merger, first with fellow Swedish car manufacturer Saab and later with French automaker Renault, the CEO of Volvo, Pehr G. Gyllenhammar, was ready to try something different. Gyllenhammar looked across the border to Norway. In 1978, he attempted to strike a deal with the Norwegian government that would offer up 40 percent of Volvo's stock in exchange for 200 million Swedish krona, the equivalent of about $80 million USD. The Norwegian government counteroffered—they did not have enough money for such a deal. The counteroffer would include 10 percent of the proceeds from the recently discovered Oseberg oil field. Gyllenhammar liked this offer; some of the shareholders of Volvo did not. In a shareholder vote, the deal managed to gain a 60 percent support rate; though it was more than half, it fell short of the required supermajority of 66 percent for the deal to be approved. Thus, the deal was rejected. When the true extent of the Oseberg oil field was revealed, it was estimated to contain about 2.3 billion barrels of oil worth somewhere in the range of $138 billion to $220 billion USD. Furthermore, the Oseberg oil Field also contained a notable amount of natural gas, which would only further increase its estimated value. Volvo would continue to struggle for the next two decades as it slowly became outsold by popular Japanese automakers such as Honda and Toyota. Eventually, Volvo would end up selling their car division off to Ford in 1999 for $6.5 billion USD, and Ford would struggle to support Volvo for the next decade. In the recovery from the Great Recession of 2008-9, during which Ford was hit hard, in an effort to raise some capital Ford decided to sell Volvo off for $1.5 billion USD, at a massive loss, to the Chinese automaker Geely in 2010.

***

In history, we see great opportunities missed by companies that, had they seized those opportunities, would have made them millions of dollars and made them the arbiters of change in the world. Although it is easy to laugh at the executives and CEOs of these companies and pass them over as being ignorant or incompetent, it is important to keep in mind the context of the situation at the time and what led to each company making a particular decision that proved to be a grave mistake. In the case of Blockbuster, the CEO was not entirely wrong when he stated that mailing DVDs to customers was a "niche" market. Keep in mind that Netflix did not begin their success in the video-streaming service for which they are known today until after Blockbuster had filed for bankruptcy. In other words, Blockbuster had been beaten by Netflix's "niche" mail-in-DVD business model alone. Blockbuster was not entirely ignorant of the onslaught of digital movie distribution services, whether through ordering DVDs online or video streaming. In leaked information from Blockbuster's internal reports in the mid-2000s, management was well-aware of the threats posed by companies such as Netflix. Where they failed was simply on a single point: management was under the false impression that things were going to stay the same; they believed that what had worked in the past would continue to work in the future with no change. Blockbuster had been raking in millions from the old business model that involved charging customers late fees. Why rock the boat? We see this theme come up again in the story of Yahoo! versus Google. From a business standpoint, perhaps we might empathize with the executives at Yahoo! at the time. Yahoo! was making millions from running banner ads. Why spend time and money focusing on search when it seemed like it was inherently unprofitable and reduced the amount of time people spent watching banner ads. Why rock the boat? They did not truly understand the influence that this new technology would have, and by the time they realized this, it was too late. As humans we are much more prone to engage in short-term thinking rather than long-term thinking. This short-term thinking and need for instant gratification is reflected in the Volvo story. In this case, the CEO of Volvo understood the potential opportunity that lay ahead. Some of the shareholders, however, were more concerned with getting an instant cash payment, and they walked away from massive long-term gains in the future as a result. As an individual, you may never get an opportunity to have a watershed moment that changes history, but there will be similar moments that influence the outcome of your own life. You will have your own watershed moments. And, if you recognize these moments and the opportunities that lie ahead, sacrificing immediate short-term gains in exchange for long-term gains, you will become very rich, very fast.

IMPOSSIBLE ODDS VS. THE HUMAN SPIRIT

I'm often amazed by some people's ability to deal with tough situations. In my university days, one of my friends was an international student from Vietnam. He was in my program, and he took many of the same advanced math courses as I did. His tuition bill was over $30,000 per semester because he was an international student—this was an amount easily triple what I paid as a domestic student. To make ends meet, he got a job that involved him picking earthworms (apparently, earthworms are used for things such as cosmetics and fish bait) at a farm that was a three-hour drive away. He would finish classes, start on his assignments, leave the house at 10p.m., and arrive at the farm at around 1a.m. He would pick worms for a couple hours and then be driven back just in time to see the sunrise. If he didn't have 8:30a.m. classes that day, he might catch up on a bit of sleep, but otherwise he would go straight to class. He got maybe four hours of scattered sleep each night. He would eat one can of salmon per day to further save money. Somehow, his grade point average was still higher than mine, and I didn't have any other commitments besides school at the time. Thinking about my friend's experiences, I would like to believe that I could've handled it if the roles were reversed, but honestly speaking, I'm not quite sure. I think the experiences I've just described would break most people. Sometimes, in life, you may find that you've landed yourself in a situation where the odds of achieving your goals seem impossible. You may feel like you are broken already; you may want to cry or just give up. The following are a few more stories of the amazing power of the human spirit to simply endure when the entire world crashes down.

Elon Musk vs. The World

In the summer of 2008, Elon Musk, the famous entrepreneur who had founded two famous companies, was in deep trouble. Musk had made his fortune in the early 2000s when Paypal, a company that he had cofounded, was sold to eBay. The sale of Paypal netted Musk an estimated $168 million USD. For most people, it would have been satisfactory to kick back and relax for the rest of their lives with that kind of money. Instead, Musk decided to reinvest all the money into two companies: Tesla Motors and SpaceX. In 2008, Tesla, the electric car company that he had taken over, was bleeding cash. The company only had one product, the Tesla Roadster, which had been delayed again and again due to production issues. Although interest had been high and preorders had rolled in steadily when it was first announced, some customers were beginning to become impatient; they began to withdraw their orders after multiple delivery delays over the course of years. The court of public opinion was also vehemently against Tesla. Most blogs and newspaper articles were counting the days before Tesla would go bankrupt. The popular British car-review show *Top Gear* had given the Roadster an abysmal review. Tesla was burning through about $4 million USD a month. Musk's problems did not end there; SpaceX, a company that Musk had created for building and launching rockets, had experienced three back-to-back failed launches of its Falcon 1 rocket. A fourth launch was scheduled, but Musk knew that if this launch failed again there would not be a fifth. To add insult to injury, Musk was going through a messy divorce, and in late September 2008, shortly before the scheduled fourth SpaceX rocket launch, the world was rocked by the news of the collapse of one of the world's biggest financial institutions—Lehman Brothers. This was the beginning of the Great Recession, and funding became even harder to find. Musk was selling his personal assets in an attempt to raise money. He had already devoted $70 million to Tesla and $100 million to SpaceX, and Musk was now staring down the barrel of personal bankruptcy if both companies were to fail. The preparation for the fourth launch of the SpaceX Falcon 1 rocket went anything but smoothly. The engineers had forgotten to account for the change in air pressure the rocket would experience on its air shipment to the launch site in Kwaj, and part of the rocket's body had crumpled. The estimated damage was thought to require at least 3 months to repair, which was time that SpaceX did not have. Musk quickly ordered repair parts to be sent in and a makeshift hangar was set up. The rocket ended up taking only two weeks to repair. On September 28, 2008, the Falcon 1 successfully launched, and SpaceX became the first private company to successfully launch a rocket into orbit around the Earth. However, despite the jubilation of the successful Falcon 1 launch, Musk was not in the clear yet. He still faced the possibility of having to choose which company he wanted to save. If he split his money between the two, both companies could fail. If he gave all the money to one company, the other would certainly fail. By early December, Musk finally managed to cobble $20 million together, with another $20 million from other investors. With days to go before SpaceX would go bankrupt, on December 23, 2008, Musk received the news that SpaceX had been awarded a contract from NASA to resupply the International Space Station, a contract valued at about $1.6 billion. The very next day, on Christmas Eve Day of 2008, the funding deal for Tesla was finalized, mere hours before Tesla was going to run out of cash. As of late 2019, Tesla and SpaceX are valued at about $41 billion and $33 billion respectively.

The Iron Will of Sir Ernest Shackleton

"Men wanted for hazardous journey. Low wages, bitter cold, long hours of complete darkness. Safe return doubtful. Honour and recognition in event of success." These words were an ad printed by Ernest Shackleton in a London newspaper in 1901, hoping to recruit a crew for a perilous expedition to the Antarctic. In what was perhaps a reflection of the culture and spirit of exploration in Britain at the time, over 3000 people responded to the ad. A few years later, ready for a new challenge, Shackleton assembled a crew for his expedition aboard the *Nimrod*, the first voyage that he would lead as captain, with the intention of reaching the geographic South Pole. Although he was ultimately not successful in achieving this objective, Shackleton had set a record for the farthest southern latitude ever reached by humans at the time. The way back, though, was anything but easy. Shackleton and his crew were in a race against starvation and the bitter cold. Everyone's rations had been cut to just one small biscuit per day. What kept the crew going during these hard times was Shackleton's unwavering determination and his ability to boost other people's morale. Upon seeing one of his comrades, Frank Wild, sick and on the brink of death, Shackleton offered his only daily biscuit to Wild. Wild survived the journey and later wrote in his diary, "All the money that was ever minted would not have bought that biscuit and the remembrance of that sacrifice will never leave me." Shackleton, however, was less sentimental in his diary entry describing his experience. In his diary, Shackleton simply wrote, "Difficulties are just things to overcome after all."

After returning to England, Shackleton was given a knighthood by King Edward VII. Hoping to cash in on some of his newfound fame, he invested much of his money into business ventures, including a tobacco company, a stamp-selling company, and a Hungarian mine. Unfortunately, none of these investments proved successful, and Shackleton quickly came into some financial difficulties. More pressing than his lack of success in the business world, Shackleton retained a burning desire for another expedition to the Antarctic, a fact that he kept hidden from his wife for as long as he could. This desire to go back to the Antarctic was only exacerbated by Norway's successful expedition to the geographic South Pole in late 1911. This was the original intention of his *Nimrod* expedition and a goal he had almost died in order to achieve, but still failed to realize.

Shackleton's dream materialized in his plans for the Imperial Trans-Antarctic Expedition. The goal was to cross the entire continent of Antarctica. If this feat were achieved, it would be the first of its kind in human history. Securing funding for this expedition proved difficult; the entirety of Europe at the time was bracing itself for a conflict that would eventually spiral into the World War I. Eventually, though, Shackleton was able to find enough investors to finally set sail in August 1914, just five days after the outbreak of the World War I. The ship that Shackleton chose was the Norwegian-built *Polaris*, which he renamed the *Endurance*, after his family motto: "By endurance, we conquer."

Ironically, the *Endurance* did not endure. The ship became trapped in ice, and Shackleton was forced to concede that they would be trapped on the ship for the coming winter. Shackleton knew inherently that although the situation was bad, what was even more dangerous than the bitter cold and lack of supplies was the dwindling morale of his men. To combat this, he drew up a roster of activities and assigned each person to his own duties for the day, switching the duties up often so that nobody would get stuck doing the same thing repeatedly. But despite

Shackleton's and his crew's best efforts, the ship was being squeezed on all sides by ice and faced the risk of imploding. It soon became clear that the *Endurance* had to be abandoned. Shackleton and his crew became trapped on an ice floe that was getting smaller by the day. They had salvaged three lifeboats from the Endurance, and with all other options exhausted, Shackleton ordered his men to get on the lifeboats and set sail for land. They eventually ended up on Elephant Island. To the crew and Shackleton, this might have seemed like a victory at first—they were now on solid land for the first time in 16 months. However, a deeper assessment of the situation showed that they were not yet home free. Elephant Island is nothing but a rock in the middle of the ocean. There are no people or animals, no food rations or even vegetation. They could not survive on Elephant Island for long. Shackleton was forced to commit to one of the most daring actions ever attempted by any person in history. He split the crew up, took one lifeboat for himself and five other men whom he had selected, and attempted to sail for South Georgia Island—approximately 800 miles northeast. The chances that they would survive were slim, but doing nothing would mean certain death. Along the way, Shackleton and his five-man crew encountered a storm that threatened to sink them before finally landing on South Georgia Island. When they arrived, the men all collapsed on the beach due to exhaustion. As if God had wanted to play one last trick on them, the only civilization on the island was a small whaling town on the north side of the island. Shackleton and his crew had landed on the south side, and getting to the town involved traversing 32 miles of unmapped mountainous terrain. Shackleton and his men made the journey in 36 hours and arrived at the whaling town. When they arrived, the men's physical condition could only be described as shells of what they once were. Shackleton knocked on the door of the whaling station's manager, with whom he was well-acquainted and had spent some time with years earlier. The manager did not recognize Shackleton until the latter reminded him of his name. With the immediate danger of death averted for himself, Shackleton quickly turned his attention back to rescuing the men whom he had left on Elephant Island. The Chilean Government lent Shackleton a small ship, and on the fourth rescue attempt, Shackleton managed to rescue the men still stuck on the island. Amazingly, every single person who had set sail on the *Endurance* survived. Thanks to Shackleton's extraordinary perseverance, he had managed to save every single crew member on the doomed Imperial Trans-Antarctic Expedition.

***

You will hopefully never be in a situation where you are facing personal bankruptcy while the companies you've spent your life building are melting away before your eyes, and it is unlikely that you will ever be stuck in Antarctica in the bitter cold with no food. Still, the key takeaway from these stories is the power of the human spirit in seemingly impossible circumstances. When SpaceX's rockets kept blowing up, many of the engineers broke down in tears. They had spent years planning and agonizing over the smallest details; they had turned down social interaction and sacrificed time that could otherwise have been spent with friends or family in order to work on the project. Some had dedicated most of their adult lives until then to achieve their dream of launching rockets. All it took was for one variable that went unaccounted for to cause the rockets to fail. Elon Musk must have known the frustration and experienced the hopelessness just as much as any engineer at SpaceX. When the rockets failed, there must have been moments when Musk had wanted to give up. Musk not only persevered but also encouraged others to try again and hang on even when it seemed like all had been lost. We see this spirit again in Ernest Shackleton. Shackleton correctly deduced that if they were to die on this expedition, it would not be because of the harsh environment but due to imploding morale. Shackleton knew that if he showed any signs of wavering, or even allowed the spirit of anyone else in his crew to waver, all would be lost. These stories show that sometimes, in life, if one wants something to happen badly enough, it may just be possible to simply will it into being with enough determination. By all logic and from a probabilistic standpoint, SpaceX and Tesla should have failed, but they didn't. Shackleton and his crew should not have survived, but they did. Although you may not encounter circumstances even remotely similar to those just described, it is more than likely that at some point in your life, you will encounter a goal that you would like to achieve in which the odds are stacked against you. This could be trying to get a job, building your own business, or fighting against a health problem. Whatever it may be, keep in mind the power of the human spirit and its ability to change outcomes and influence reality.

Appendix: Math Stuffs

For the extra curious, here is a collection of some of the mathematics that powers the financial world. I will go through some derivations and try to explain the math in simple terms. While it is certainly not necessary to understand any of these topics to achieve financial independence, this section gives those interested in exploring the inner mechanics of money a general idea of how things work. Keep in mind that this is by no means meant to be an exhaustive list; whole courses in universities all around the world have been created on any one of these given topics.

INTEREST AND BONDS

Earlier, we covered what interest is at its essence and why it exists in the first place. Hopefully, by now you have an idea of the power of compound interest and how to leverage it to help you achieve your financial goals. We now look at the mathematics behind how this works. To start off, let's define some variables:

$$r = Interest\ rate\ (expressed\ as\ a\ decimal)$$

$$n = Time\ period$$

$$c = Cash\ amount$$

Let's begin with simple interest. Simple interest is when you only earn interest on the principal amount of money you contributed. Meaning, the amount of money paid out is always constant, and you do not earn interest on top of your interest. The equation for this is simple because it is only a multiplicative relationship. Thus:

$Simple\ Interest = c_0 rn$, where c_0 is the principal amount of money you started off with

In real life, you will more likely encounter compound interest. This is when you earn interest on top of your previous interest payments. This works great for you if you're the investor but not so great if you're the borrower. Compound interest is the reason why a small amount of credit card debt can quickly snowball out of control, but it is also why the wealth of billionaire investors such as Warren Buffett just keeps on increasing.

If you start off with some principal amount, c_0, and then earn an interest rate of r on your principal for just one time period (i.e., n = 1), then the amount you will have at the end of the period is simply:

$$c_0(1+r)$$

But after another period (i.e., n = 2) since you will earn interest at the rate of r on top of your first period's interest, you would need to multiply the equation above by (1+r), again:

$$c_0(1+r)(1+r) = c_0(1+r)^2$$

Assuming that your rate r is expressed at an appropriate rate that matches the period of interest (i.e., an annual rate, with each period referring to one year), then, in general, the amount you will have after n periods will be:

$$c_0(1+r)^n$$

With this in mind, we can calculate the future value of an amount of money. Suppose you start off with $1,000 and you want to know how much this amount will be worth in 10 years compounded annually at a rate of 8 percent per year. The calculation would then be:

$$Future\ Value\ (FV) = c_0(1+r)^n = 1000(1+0.08)^{10} = 2158.92$$

Note that sometimes the rate at which a rate is compounded will not match the time period in which the interest rate is given. For example, an investment may compound twice a year (semiannually), but you are given a yearly interest rate. In this case, you will have to adjust the formula to reflect this. If you start off with an annual rate and you wish to adjust it to find the FV for different types of compounding, you will have to divide your interest rate by the number of periods and multiply the exponent by the appropriate number of periods your interest rate is compounded for. The formula for the adjustment is as follows:

$$Future\ Value\ (FV) = c_0 \left(1 + \frac{r}{n}\right)^{tn}$$

In this formula, t represents the time in years. So, if your interest rate is an annual figure but you want to calculate the FV for semiannual compounding, then n = 2, since there are two semiannual periods in one year. Similarly, for monthly compounding, n = 12.

For example, if you wanted to calculate the future value of a dollar 10 years from now, compounded semiannually at an annual rate of 5 percent, the equation reads:

$$Future\ Value\ (FV) = c_0 \left(1 + \frac{r}{n}\right)^{tn} = \left(1 + \frac{0.05}{2}\right)^{(10)(2)} = 1.6386$$

It is interesting to note that if we increase the compounding frequency, the future value goes up. Doing the same calculation as above but with monthly compounding, the calculation becomes:

$$Future\ Value\ (FV) = c_0 \left(1 + \frac{r}{n}\right)^{tn} = \left(1 + \frac{0.05}{12}\right)^{(10)(12)} = 1.6470$$

This makes intuitive sense, since by increasing the compounding frequency (for example, from every year to every month), you earn interest faster. If we take the limit as n goes to infinity, meaning we take the compounding period to be arbitrarily small, we can show this using a commonly known identity:

$$\lim_{n \to \infty} \left(1 + \frac{r}{n}\right)^{tn} = e^{rt}$$

This means that if n is arbitrarily large (meaning that we increase the frequency of compounding to infinity), we get:

$$Future\ Value\ (FV) = c_0 e^{rt}$$

Taking the previous example but with continuous compounding, we get:

$$Future\ Value\ (FV) = c_0 e^{rt} = (1)(e)^{(0.05)(10)} = 1.6487$$

This represents the best-case scenario for a compounded rate of return if your goal is to maximize the future value of your money in a given amount of time.

Present Value

The equation for future value can be rearranged to "discount" a future value back to its present value. This means that if you know an appropriate interest rate to discount a future value by, you may bring it back to what it is worth in today's money. For example, if you believe that inflation will be on average about 2 percent per year for the next 20 years, and you want to know how much $1 million in 20 years from now is worth today, adjusted for inflation, then the calculation will be:

$$Present\ Value\ (PV) = \frac{c_0}{(1+r)^n} = \frac{1,000,000}{(1+0.02)^{20}} = 627,971.33$$

So, we can conclude that the value of $1 million in 20 years is roughly just over $600,000 today if inflation is about 2 percent per year.

We can modify the equation for present value to account for situations where you may have cash flows coming in at different times throughout a longer period of time. This will be the case if you hold a bond, where you get regular bond payments coming in at different times. In general, if this is the case, the equation will be:

$$PV(c) = c_0 + \frac{c_1}{(1+r)} + \frac{c_2}{(1+r)^2} + \cdots + \frac{c_n}{(1+r)^n}$$

A bond essentially comprises two parts: the regular, fixed coupon payments, sometimes called the "annuity," and the payment of the face value when the bond matures, sometimes called the "lump sum." The value of the bond, then, is the sum of these two parts, and this sum can be calculated for any given fixed interest rate r.

Since a bond has fixed coupon payments, we can fix the c in the above equation. (i.e., $c = c_1 = c_2 = \ldots = c_n$). With some algebra, we can simplify the sum into something more digestible. Therefore, the annuity part is:

$$\sum \frac{c}{(1+r)^n} = \frac{c}{1+r} + \cdots + \frac{c}{(1+r)^N}$$

$$= \frac{c}{1+r}\left(1 + \frac{1}{1+r} + \cdots + \frac{1}{(1+r)^{N-1}}\right)$$

$$= \frac{c}{1+r} \times \frac{1 - \left(\frac{1}{1+r}\right)^N}{1 - \frac{1}{1+r}} = c\left[\frac{1}{r}\left(1 - \frac{1}{1+r}\right)^N\right]$$

This part is sometimes called the "annuity factor," since it is used to valuate the price of the annuity portion of the bond. The present value

PAGE 193

of the face value is easy to calculate, since it is just one payment after n periods.

$$Present\ Value\ of\ Face\ Value = \frac{F}{(1+r)^N}, \text{where F is the face value}$$

Putting these two parts together, we arrive at the formula for calculating the value of a bond:

$$Bond\ Value = c\left[\frac{1}{r}\left(1 - \frac{1}{1+r}\right)^N\right] + \frac{F}{(1+r)^N}$$

Once again, c is the amount of one coupon payment, F is the face value, and r is the prevailing interest rate that is used to valuate the bond.

If we define the bond value to be P, a premium bond is when P > F, the face value. A discount bond is when P < F. We say a bond is sold at par if P = F. If the coupon rate is equal to the interest rate per period, then P = F. If the coupon rate is higher than the interest rate per period, then it's a premium bond. Similarly, if the coupon rate is less than the interest rate per period, then it's a discount bond. If the bond gets sold between periods, the coupon rate gets prorated in the calculations.

CRYPTOGRAPHY AND CRYPTOCURRENCIES

To understand cryptocurrencies, we must first understand some of the math that powers them. Cryptography is defined on Wikipedia as "the practice and study of techniques for secure communication in the presence of third parties called adversaries." Most modern cryptographic theorems rely on one simple mathematical property: it is very easy to multiply large prime numbers together to get a larger composite number, but it is very difficult to decompose a large composite number into its prime factors. Recall that prime numbers are numbers that have only two factors: the number 1 and themselves. Composite numbers have more than two factors and are the product of prime numbers. For example, if you wanted to represent the number 12 with prime numbers, you can begin to break it down into 3*4. However, 4 is a composite number, since it is equal to 2*2. We can no longer break the number 2 down any further, since its only factors are 1 and 2. Therefore, 12 can be represented as: 2*2*3, a product of prime numbers. A collection of these prime numbers is called the *prime decomposition* of a composite number.

With small numbers, finding the prime decomposition is intuitive, but with large numbers (i.e., numbers with tens or even hundreds of digits) there is no easy way. This principle is useful for cryptography: we can quickly encode a message by multiplying large prime numbers together, and these large prime numbers constitute a "private key." We then send a message as the product of those numbers, called the "public key." Since it is hard to find the prime factors, it will be difficult for those who intercept the public key to guess your private key. We will now describe a cryptographic method called RSA encryption, which leverages this fact to achieve secure transmissions of information.

RSA Encryption

First, let's define a few terms. In math, the modulus operation gives the remainder of the division of two quantities. Let's call the quantity being divided a, and a divisor, m. Then we can have an operation called modulus, written as mod(a,m) whose result is the remainder when a is repeatedly divided by m. For example,

$$\text{mod}(21,5) = 1$$

That is, if we divide 21 by 5 repeatedly, the remainder is 1. Notice that in the modulus operation we do not care about exactly how many times a goes in m evenly, but only about the remainder. With that in mind, let's move on to a second definition.

Let m be a fixed positive integer. if two integers a and b have the same remainder when divided by m, they are said to be *congruent*. Formally, we write that:

$$a \equiv b \pmod{m}$$

Notice the symbol that looks like an equal sign but with three lines instead of two. This is the symbol we will use for congruence from this point forward. In plain words, the statement above simply says that a and b have the same remainder when repeatedly divided by m.

Lastly, for an integer $d > 0$, and two other integers a and b, if:

1. $\mod(a, d) = \mod(b, d) = 0$,
2. For any other integer c, where $\mod(a, c) = \mod(b, c) = 0$, we have that $d > c$

We call d the greatest common divisor of a and b. Or, more formally,

$$d = \gcd(a, b)$$

In plain words, the greatest common divisor between two integers, a and b, is simply the largest number that can evenly divide into both. For example:

$$\gcd(12, 16) = 4$$

With all this in mind, we may begin the formal process of setting up, encoding, and decoding a message using RSA.

Part 1: Setting up RSA

We choose two large and distinct prime numbers p and q (meaning $p \neq q$). We then select a number e such that:

$$\gcd(e, (p-1)(q-1)) = 1 \text{ and } 1 < e < (p-1)(q-1)$$

We then solve the equation:

$$ed \equiv 1 \pmod{(p-1)(q-1)} \text{ for some } d \text{ where } 1 \leq d \leq (p-1)(q-1)$$

And we publish the public key pair (e, pq).

We keep the private key pair (d, pq) secure. We will use this to decrypt the message later.

Part 2: Sending the Message

Suppose you want to send a message in the form of a number M. We look up the recipient's public key (e, pq) and we choose M such that:

$$0 \leq M \leq pq$$

We are now ready to compute the encrypted message (called the ciphertext) by solving the following equation:

$$M^e \equiv C \pmod{pq}, \text{ where } 0 \leq C < pq$$

We then send the ciphertext C.

Part 3: Receiving the Message

Once the recipient receives C, we use the previously computed private key pair (d, pq) to get M back. To do this, we solve for R in the following equation:

$$C^d \equiv R \pmod{pq}, \text{where } 0 \leq R < pq$$

Then, you will find that R = M. In other words, R is the original message.

Practically, the reason why RSA is difficult to crack is the computational difficulty involved in guessing the number d in the equation above. There is no easy way to solve the equation above if d is not provided. Even for computers, brute-forcing the equation to solve for d may take such a large amount of time (in the magnitude of thousands of years) that it would be impractical to do so.

An Example of RSA in Action

Let p = 9026694843092981746248479430766619417461579144393937

Let q = 7138718791169359634308025171032405888327684736583

Then,

pq = 64439036098539423089800377907005024856771034536315452625458662901646061990955188192298998039774472711

You will notice that these numbers are extremely large. This is done on purpose, since the numbers must be large in order to prevent a computer from being able to feasibly brute-force decrypt the encryption.

We now choose the number e such that:

$$ed \equiv 1 \;(\text{mod } (p-1)(q-1)), \text{for some d where } 1 \leq d \leq (p-1)(q-1)$$

We will choose e to be:

$e = $ 95735962120300597326295086957971745569558757345310234412173 1

You may use software to check that it is indeed that case that $\gcd(e, (p-1)(q-1)) = 1$

And that,

$$1 < e < (p-1)(q-1)$$

We now solve for d in the equation above:

$d = $ 5587652122635102292797952485365522717791728568267561000820111 8490306463274981250258312094640 72548779

We now publish the public key (e, pq) and keep the private key (d, pq) secure.

Let's say we wanted to encode the message M (some digits of π):

$$\text{Let } M = 3141592653$$

We now compute the ciphertext C using the equation:

$$M^e \equiv C \;(\text{mod } pq), where\; 0 \leq C < pq$$

And get:

$$C = 4006696554308081561028140198388509626485815105444152455473825\\50676593081333888622449139482537422205367$$

We send C to the recipient.

Once the recipient receives the message, we use the private key d to solve:

$$C^d \equiv R \pmod{pq}, \text{where } 0 \leq R < pq$$

And we find that

$$R = 3141592653$$

This is our original message.

The Bitcoin Protocol

We have now seen the basic idea of public- and private-key encryption. We will now go through how this concept is leveraged to create cryptocurrencies.

Imagine that you and your friends keep a list of who owes whom money, and you post that list publicly in a place that everyone can access. In essence, this is what is called a *ledger*. Since the ledger is public, a certain degree of trust needs to be established, or anyone can fraudulently claim that you or someone else owes them money. To prevent this, we need some sort of signature to ensure that party A actually agreed to send party B a specific amount of money. If this transaction is done online as opposed to real life, we would need some sort of digital signature. At first, the idea of a digital signature seems rather odd, since we usually think of a signature as a piece of text that a computer can easily copy. But, going back to what we've just learned about public and private keys, we can leverage this knowledge to create unique signatures. We will define two functions, the first being a function that will generate a signature based on both the message that one is signing and one's private key. Formally,

$$Sign(message, private\ key) = Signature$$

Then, we need a function that serves as a way to verify that the signature is correct. For this, we will use the public key:

$$Verify(message, signature, public\ key) = True\ OR\ False$$

We won't go into the mechanics of how these functions work, but just note that they are set up in such a way that there is no other method to generate a signature that would work for the *Verify* function other than brute-force guessing. If we take a 256-bit signature, a computer seeking to crack the signature would need to guess 2^{256} possibilities. This immensely large number of tries would make it completely unfeasible for any computer to guess the correct signature.

There are a few ground rules that must be followed before we can establish a proper online digital ledger. First, we need to assign a unique identification to each transaction to prevent the same transaction from being copied to the ledger multiple times. Second, one might recklessly agree to pay others large sums of money by writing transactions on the ledger without actually having the money to be able to settle all the agreed-upon transactions. We must prevent anyone from spending more money than they have, and this problem can be solved by everyone agreeing to contribute a set sum of money to the metaphorical pot in the beginning and just transacting with what's in the pot. Note that this solution would involve everyone knowing the full history of the ledger in order for one to calculate if any given person has enough ledger dollars to complete a transaction.

Theoretically, as this ledger gets longer and longer, one can just perform transactions purely using the money they possess according to the ledger. The ledger would never have to be settled in US dollars or whatever currency it started off with—the dollars that the ledger records can just be "ledger dollars"—thereby standing as a currency of its own.

There's one more problem with this ledger system: it still remains centralized, meaning that the ledger is posted in one place; everyone using the ledger would have to trust the website or authority hosting the ledger. If the host's website goes down, this will knock the entire ledger system out. We will need to decentralize this system in order to solve this problem, which involves giving everyone a copy of the ledger and letting everyone keep track of their own ledger. However, this presents a different problem: How might everyone agree on how to add a transaction to the ledger and the order in which transactions should appear?

In the Bitcoin protocol, this problem is solved using a tool called a *cryptographic hash function*. Now, the idea behind a cryptographic hash function is to generate an output of fixed length (a hash) that is based from some input or message, with the output changing in a completely unpredictable way if the input changes even slightly. One of the most popular hashing functions is called "SHA256," which produces a 256-bit number as its hash. The idea is that if one were given a SHA256 hash, there would be no feasible way to compute what input generated that hash.

With this in mind, let's say you wanted to find a number that would generate a SHA256 hash with 30 leading zeroes when you attach it to the end of the ledger. The probability that you will find such a number randomly is $1/(2^{30})$, or about 1 in a billion. Thus, you will have to make about a billion guesses before you find such a number. Once you do, however, it would be easy to check whether this number actually produces the desired output of a number with 30 leading zeroes just by running the hashing function. This number is called the *proof of work*. Note that the proof of work would produce the desired hash only for the specific copy of the ledger it is attached to. Due to the nature of the hashing function, as we mentioned earlier, if the message changes at all (even slightly), it would completely change the SHA256 hash and render the number you just computed useless.

Suppose you wanted to confirm a "block," or group, of transactions and add them to the ledger. The Bitcoin protocol sets the transactions up such that each "block" has its own proof of work (which produces a SHA256 hash with a prespecified number of leading zeroes) that is based on both the transactions that are in the block and the hash from the previous block, which has been confirmed and added to the ledger already. Thus, these blocks end up being "chained" together, since the proof of work for each block is dependent upon that of the previous block. Hence, this ledger is now known as a "blockchain." Note that this prevents any block or transaction from being changed once it has entered the blockchain, since doing so would change the SHA256 hash for every subsequent block added to the chain.

Now, adding a new block to the blockchain involves a large amount of computation, since it essentially involves brute-force guessing a number that will produce a SHA256 hash with a given number of leading zeroes, which involves combing through trillions of possibilities. To motivate people to dedicate the considerably larger amount of computational power required for this task, if a proof of work is found and a block is successfully added to the blockchain, whoever adds the block may include a line at the beginning of the block that gives them a prespecified amount of ledger dollars. This is called a "block reward," and the people trying to add to the blockchain are referred to as "miners." Being a successful miner involves racing to find the next proof of work before anyone else does in order to be the first to add this to the blockchain. Once a block is added, everyone else must start from scratch, since the proof of work required for the next block is now based on the block that had just been added. At this point, the "ledger dollar" is a cryptocurrency, and this is how Bitcoin and many other cryptocurrencies work.

THE PRISONER'S DILEMMA

Game theory involves the use of mathematical models and logical puzzles to explain collective human decision making. In this context, a "game" refers to any interaction between two or more humans. In particular, there are generally two broad categories of games: cooperative and competitive. One of the most famous examples of a competitive game, in which participants work against each other and try to "win" for themselves, is the prisoner's dilemma:

1. Consider two individuals, Alice and Bob, who both have been arrested for a crime that they had committed together.
2. The police has enough evidence to give Alice and Bob each a 2-year prison sentence if no one confesses to the crime.
3. As part of a plea deal, if Alice agrees to rat Bob out, she will go free, and Bob will receive 10 years in prison.

4. The same plea deal is offered to Bob; if he rats Alice out, he will go free, and Alice will receive 10 years in prison.
5. If both Alice and Bob rat each other out, they will each receive 5 years in prison.
6. Alice and Bob are not allowed to communicate or coordinate with each other before making the decision of whether to rat the other person out. They must both arrive at their own decisions independently.

We can summarize the outcomes in a table:

Alice/Bob	Blame Other Person	Stay Silent
Blame Other Person	5 years, 5 years	0 years, 10 years
Stay Silent	10 years, 0 years	2 years, 2 years

Table 4: Decision Matrix for the Prisoner's Dilemma

Note that, as table 4 suggests, the best outcome overall is for both parties to stay silent, in which case they would each get two years of prison time.

Of course, in reality, human behavior is rather complex, and it would be hard to definitively say what each person will do. For the sake of concision, let's explore a suggested sequence of resulting events under the assumptions of Game Theory.

Game Theory

The study of mathematical models of strategic interaction among rational decision-makers

Game Theory was pioneered as an independent field of study in the late 1920s, and it attempts to logically map out the outcome of any given interaction between two or more parties (known as a "game") given that the participants behave rationally. The aforementioned Prisoner's Dilemma was first invented as a thought experiment by mathematicians Merrill M. Flood and Melvin Dresher as part of their work for the RAND corporation for possible applications of these principles to global nuclear strategy.

According to the assumptions of Game Theory, both parties will blame each other and end up each serving five years in prison. This is because the scenario in which they both blame each other is what's called the Nash equilibrium. Let's analyze further why this is the case.

Notice that without the ability to communicate or coordinate, one party has no idea what the other party will do and must act in a way that prioritizes their own self-interest. If you are Alice, you do not know what Bob would do; if you blame Bob and he stays silent, you go free. If you blame Bob and he blames you back, you get 5 years, which is still better than the 10 years you risk getting if he blames you and you stay silent. You are compelled to blame Bob because you feel the need to protect yourself, and you have no way of trusting that Bob will not blame you. Meanwhile, Bob is thinking the same thing. Thus, we find that both prisoners blame each other, and both end up serving 5 years.

This simple thought exercise can explain why human decision-making can create suboptimal situations overall, even though it may seem like individuals are making optimal decisions for themselves. It can explain why, for example, there has been so little action on combating climate change. If one country commits to sacrificing a bit of its economy in exchange for action on climate change, they will lose out to countries that do not sacrifice their economies and do nothing about climate change. Each country can choose between the risk of taking an economic hit by imposing carbon taxes and cutting back on fossil fuels, or they can do nothing and wait for someone else to take the hit first. From an individualistic, rational standpoint, it would appear that doing nothing is the correct course of action. Overall, however, if everyone plays the same *game* and everyone elects to do nothing, waiting for someone else to take the hit first, we are stuck with the unfavorable outcome of worsening climate change overall due to a lack of action. On a more positive note, game theory provides some evidence of how the stock market can be inefficient, since human behavior can lead to suboptimal outcomes. This is a good thing for investors, who seek to exploit the inefficiencies of the market for potential financial gain.

LINEAR PROGRAMS AND OPTIMIZATION

Sometimes, in life, we encounter situations in which we want to maximize or minimize a value based on some constraints. For example, if you are the head of a manufacturing facility, you may want to know how many units of a series of products to produce, with the goal of maximizing profit given the cost of the materials and labor, subject to a certain necessary amount of machine hours for each product. Another example: say you are scheduling a series of sports teams for a championship and you would like to minimize the amount of consecutive away games any given sports team plays, in order to minimize travel fatigue. However, the constraints in this case may be that each team is required to play a certain number of games against any other team, and that a team cannot be an "away" team more than a prespecified number of times (being an "away" team will require travel, and the goal here is to minimize travel for teams). These problems can be modeled mathematically, and solving these problems involves a concept known as *optimization*, a process that seeks to find the "optimal" value of a problem by either minimizing or maximizing an "objective function" subject to a series of constraints. We will detail the process of just one type of optimization problem, called a "linear program." As the name suggests, in a linear program both the constraints and the objective function are linear. This means that the objective function takes on the form:

$$f(x) = a^T x$$

Where x is a vector of dimension n, and a contains the associated scalars of x.

An example of a linear function:

$$f(x) = x_1 - x_2 + 3x_3$$

Here is an example of what is *not* a linear function:

$$f(x) = x_1 + 2x_2 + 6x_3 x_4$$

What makes this function not linear is the product between x_3 and x_4; this makes the function no longer linear.

For our constraints, we also want linear constraints. A constraint is said to be linear if it follows one of the forms:

$$f(x) = \beta \text{ or } f(x) \leq \beta \text{ or } f(x) \geq \beta$$

In which *f(x)* is a linear function and β is a real number. Note that the inequalities here must be either "greater than or equal to" or "less than or equal to." For example, this is not a linear constraint:

$$x_1 - x_2 + 3x_3 < 3$$

An Example of Optimization

The following example is from *A Gentle Introduction to Optimization* by Guenin et al. Suppose we receive the following information about a series of products that require machine hours and labor to produce:

Product	Machine 1 (hrs)	Machine 2 (hrs)	Skilled Labor (hrs)	Unskilled Labor (hrs)	Unit Sale Price ($)
1	11	4	8	7	300
2	7	6	5	8	260
3	6	5	5	7	220
4	5	4	6	4	180

Table 5: Required Machine and Labor Hours and Price per Product

Suppose further that:

1. Each month, 700 hours are available on Machine 1 and 500 hours are available on Machine 2
2. Up to 600 hours of skilled labor is available at $8 per hour
3. Up to 650 hours of unskilled labor is available at $6 per hour

We want to determine how much of each product to produce with the intention of maximizing profit (defined as the difference between revenue and cost).

First, let's define the variables x_1, x_2, x_3, x_4 which represent the amount of each product (numbered 1 to 4) to produce. We also need the variables y_s, y_u to denote how many skilled or unskilled hours we need to buy, with y_s standing for skilled labor and y_u for unskilled labor.

Now, let's define our objective function, which would be the total profit (which we are trying to maximize).

Total Profit:

$$300x_1 + 260x_2 + 220x_3 + 180x_4 - (8y_s + 6y_u)$$

The former part is the revenue we will make from each product, while the latter part in parentheses is the cost of labor required to produce all of the products.

Next, we need to implement our constraints. First, note that we only have 700 hours of time available on Machine 1. Using the time required for each product for Machine 1 in table 5, we have:

$$11x_1 + 7x_2 + 6x_3 + 5x_4 \leq 700$$

Similarly, we have a similar constraint for Machine 2:

$$4x_1 + 6x_2 + 5x_3 + 4x_4 \leq 500$$

We must now also make sure that we purchase enough skilled and unskilled labor to ensure the products are produced. The following two constraints will enforce this:

$$8x_1 + 5x_2 + 5x_3 + 6x_4 \leq y_s$$

$$7x_1 + 8x_2 + 7x_3 + 4x_4 \leq y_u$$

We also have the constraint that we can only purchase up to 600 hours of skilled labor and 650 hours of unskilled labor. Simply put:

$$y_s \leq 600$$

$$y_u \leq 650$$

Finally, we need a constraint that states we cannot use a negative number of labor hours or produce a negative quantity of products. Therefore, all variables must be nonnegative.

$$x_1, x_2, x_3, x_4, y_s, y_u \geq 0$$

Putting it altogether, we get the following formulation:

$$max\ (300x_1 + 260x_2 + 220x_3 + 180x_4 - (8y_s + 6y_u))$$

Subject to

$$11x_1 + 7x_2 + 6x_3 + 5x_4 \leq 700$$

$$4x_1 + 6x_2 + 5x_3 + 4x_4 \leq 500$$

$$8x_1 + 5x_2 + 5x_3 + 6x_4 \leq y_s$$

$$7x_1 + 8x_2 + 7x_3 + 4x_4 \leq y_u$$

$$y_s \leq 600$$

$$y_u \leq 650$$

$$x_1, x_2, x_3, x_4, y_s, y_u \geq 0$$

We will not go through how to solve LPs, since this is beyond the scope of this book. However, just note that there are very efficient computer programs that can not only do the calculations for you but also prove from a mathematical standpoint why a particular answer is optimal. In general, sometimes it may be the case that a problem has no possible solution. When this happens, the problem is said to be *infeasible*. There are also cases where a problem has no optimal solution—for example, if you are trying to maximize a value and the constraints allow the value of the objective function to get arbitrarily large. In this case, the problem is said to be *unbounded*.

About the Author

Andy Zhou graduated from the University of Waterloo in Ontario, Canada, in 2019 with an bachelor's degree in mathematics (honors). Throughout his time at university, he took on various internships at many major Canadian companies, including the Royal Bank of Canada and Loblaw. In October 2016, he enrolled in the university's official stock simulator game, StockTrak run by the Faculty of Mathematics. By the time of his graduation, Andy ranked fifth out of 535 participants, with a total portfolio net return of 98 percent. In the last year of university prior to his graduation, he founded and led the UW FIRE Club, where he led discussions and debates on all topics related to finance and investing. He also runs his own investment portfolio using money that he saved from his internships. Between 2014 and 2019, he managed to build up a portfolio valued at over $20,000 CAD with a trailing twelve-month return of over 60 percent at the time of this writing.

As well as writing in his spare time, Andy is also an avid reader. In early 2019 he founded the UW Book Club, where he led discussions on both fiction and nonfiction books. In this debut book, *Financial Independence Theory*, Andy hopes to leverage a combination of the knowledge and experiences gained from both his university lectures and real scenarios in workplaces to create a formal methodology of getting good at personal finance and achieving financial independence.

Currently, Andy works and resides in Toronto; he works for Grizzle.com, a startup that focuses on investment research and providing beginner investors with clear, intuitive, and accurate information rather than the jargon-heavy reports and articles prevalent in the financial products and investments industry.

For questions regarding this book, Andy can be reached on Twitter at @andyquanzhou.

References

3Blue1Brown. 2017. "But How Does Bitcoin Actually Work?" July 7, 2017. https://www.youtube.com/watch?v=bBC-nXj3Ng4.

Guenin, B., Könemann J., and Tuncel, L. 2015. *A Gentle Introduction to Optimization*. Cambridge, UK: Cambridge University Press.

Kiyosaki, R. T. 2017. *Rich Dad Poor Dad: With Updates for Today's World and 9 New Study Session Sections*. Scottsdale, AZ: Plata.

MacAskill, W. 2016. *Doing Good Better: Effective Altruism and a Radical New Way to Make a Difference*. London: Guardian Faber.

McMillan, L. G. 2012. *Options as a Strategic Investment*. 5th ed. New York: Prentice Hall.

Thoughty2. 2018. "These Men Should Have Died, So How Did They Survive?" December 20, 2018. https://www.youtube.com/watch?v=HhgK_1oGSVw.

Town, P. 2006. *Rule #1: The Simple Strategy for Successful Investing in Only 15 Minutes a Week!* New York: Crown.

Vance, A. 2017. *Elon Musk: Tesla, SpaceX, and the Quest for a Fantastic Future*. New York: Ecco.

Wall Street Journal. 2018. "Why Warren Buffett Said No to Lehman and AIG in 2008." September 7, 2018. https://www.youtube.com/watch?v=1QeUcfqkUzc.

www.ingramcontent.com/pod-product-compliance
Lightning Source LLC
Chambersburg PA
CBHW032224080426

42735CB00008B/706